GENERAL SIR ARTHUR WELLESLEY, K.P., 1803.

INTRODUCTION.

——•◦•——

WHEN the proposal for a series of republications in book form of some of the more important articles and short stories appearing in the pages of the *Pall Mall Magazine* was first made to us by Mr. R. B. Marston, we accepted it without hesitation, perceiving at once that an admirable medium would thus be provided by which much valuable literary matter might be made known to an even wider circle of the public than the readers of the periodical of which we have the conduct. Field-Marshal Viscount Wolseley's graphic and analytical papers on the "Decline and Fall of Napoleon," which constitute the first volume of the PALL MALL MAGAZINE LIBRARY, achieved, as we are able to say from personal knowledge, a very remarkable success not only in England and America, but on the Continent ; especially in Paris, where they were translated and published in book form. Much the same may be said with regard to General Lord Roberts' valuable and instructive articles on the "Rise of Wellington," which found especial favour with military readers in all branches of the Service, and we have reason to think that the collection of these into a single and handy volume will meet with the general approval of military men, and might form a valuable text-book for military students. The articles commenced by Viscount Wolseley and continued by Lord Roberts are now being followed in the pages of the *Pall Mall Magazine* by Lieut.-General Sir Evelyn Wood's papers on " Cavalry in the Waterloo Campaign," and we hope from time to time to be able to secure other able military writers as contributors to deal with subjects having an equal historical interest. We conclude by saying that the Publishers have our hearty sympathy and will have our lively co-operation in the publication of the PALL MALL MAGAZINE LIBRARY, and so far as lies in our power we shall endeavour to assist them in making each successive volume such as to entitle it to a foremost place in the literature of the day.

FREDERICK HAMILTON.
DOUGLAS STRAIGHT.

Editors *Pall Mall Magazine.*

18, CHARING CROSS ROAD.
March, 1895.

LIST OF ILLUSTRATIONS.

————◦◦◦————

THE

RISE OF WELLINGTON.

———◇———

"The foremost quality in a general is that he shall
have a cool head, which receives just impressions of
things; which is never confused, nor allows itself to
be dazzled or thrown off its balance by good or bad
news."—NAPOLEON.

———

CHAPTER I.

THE military career of Wellington naturally divides
itself into three periods—the Indian period, the
Peninsular period, and the period during which he
commanded the Allied Forces in the Netherlands,
terminating in the battle of Waterloo. I propose,
therefore, in three chapters, relating in turn to each of
these periods, briefly to describe the principal inci-
dents of this great soldier's life, and to show how the
experience he gained first in the East, and afterwards
in South-Western Europe, so developed his natural

B

talents and administrative capacity that he was finally able to meet and overthrow the French Emperor, whose genius for war had up to that date been regarded as absolutely unrivalled.

Arthur Wellesley, the fourth son of the first Earl of Mornington, was born in 1769, and was educated first at a private school in Chelsea, and subsequently for a short time at Eton, whence he was removed to a military college at Angers, in France, presided over by an engineer officer, the Marquis of Pignerol. Being looked upon as the dunce of the family, and described by his mother as being " food for powder and nothing more," it was determined, according to the custom of those days, to provide him with a livelihood in the army, and at the age of seventeen he obtained an ensigncy in the 41st Foot. His family interest being powerful, he was rapidly promoted, becoming a lieutenant after nine months' service as ensign, a captain after three-and-a-half years' service as lieutenant, a major after less than two years' service as captain, a lieutenant-colonel after five months' service as major, and a colonel at the age of twenty-seven, after less than three years' service as lieutenant-colonel. He was attached to the cavalry as well as the infantry, being transferred from the 41st Foot to the 12th Light Dragoons, thence to the

76th Foot, the 18th Light Dragoons, and finally to the 33rd Foot, of which he obtained the command in 1793.

While stationed at home he sat in the Irish House of Commons as member for Trim, and was also for some time aide-de-camp to the Lord-Lieutenant of Ireland.

In 1794 he accompanied his regiment to Antwerp, where it joined the force under the command of the Duke of York, and took part in the movement on Breda, and the engagement at Boxtel, a village on the river Dommel. On this occasion Lieutenant-Colonel Wellesley behaved with conspicuous judgment and gallantry—so much so, in fact, that he attracted the favourable notice of General Dundas, who afterwards entrusted him with the duty of covering the retreat of the British army. This retreat was conducted under great difficulties by Count Walmoden, a Hanoverian general, to whom the Duke of York had handed over his command; and after suffering the most grievous hardships and privations during the winter of 1794–95, the troops reached Bremen and re-embarked for England early in 1795. This first experience of field service was, no doubt, extremely valuable to Wellington in after years. It must have taught him that soldiers even of the best quality, well drilled, disciplined and equipped, cannot hope to be successful unless proper arrangements are made for their supply and transport; and unless those who direct the operations have formed some definite plan of action, and have sufficient zeal and professional knowledge to carry it out. If the French generals had taken full advantage of the opportunities which the incapacity of the English and German commanders threw in their way, the British force must have been annihilated. As it was, Wellington considered it "a marvel that any one belonging to the force escaped."

On its return to England Lieutenant-Colonel Wellesley's regiment was quartered at Warley, while he proceeded on leave to Ireland. Apparently disgusted at the mismanagement of the troops employed in the Low Countries, he made up his mind to leave the army, and in June 1795 applied to Lord Camden, then Lord-Lieutenant of Ireland, for a civil post under the Irish Government. He wrote: "You will probably be surprised at my desiring a civil instead of a military office. It is certainly a departure from the line which I prefer; but I see the manner in which the military offices are filled, and I don't wish to ask you for that which I know you cannot give me." This application was unsuccessful;

and in the autumn of the same year Wellesley's regiment was ordered to join in an expedition directed against the French settlements in the West Indies. The ships in which the troops embarked were driven back by stress of weather to Spithead, and the proposed operations being abandoned, the 33rd Foot was landed and quartered at Poole. A few months later the regiment was ordered to India, and arrived in Calcutta in February 1797. Shortly after Colonel Wellesley had reached India, the Governor-General, Sir John Shore, offered him the command of an expedition which was intended for the capture of Manilla; and, all the necessary arrangements being complete, the troops embarked and proceeded as far as Penang. Owing, however, to apprehensions of danger within India itself, the force was recalled, and Colonel Wellesley returned to Calcutta, whence he started early in 1798 on a visit to Lord Hobart, the Governor of Madras. Two months later Lord Mornington, Wellesley's eldest brother, replaced Sir John Shore as Governor-General, and at once took into consideration the critical state of affairs in Mysore, where Tippoo Sultan, the son of Hyder Ali, continued his late father's fanatical animosity towards the English, and had allied himself with the French Republic, hoping for its aid in attacking the East India Company's possessions in Southern India.

The first step to be taken by the Governor-General was to secure the friendship, or at any rate the neutrality, of the Nizam, and for this purpose it was essential to re-establish British influence at that ruler's court, and induce him to consent to the disbandment of a portion of his troops which had become formidable owing to its being officered by Frenchmen. This precautionary measure was successfully accomplished, and a fresh treaty of alliance was entered into between the Nizam and the Government of India in 1798; the French officers in the Nizam's service were dismissed and sent home; the force to which they belonged was broken up, and a subsidiary force, 6000 strong, under British officers, took its place. While all this was going on Wellesley had been sent with his regiment from Calcutta to Madras, and on his arrival at the capital of the Southern Presidency, he undertook, in communication with Lord Clive, the Governor, and General Harris, the Commander-in-Chief, to organise the commissariat, transport, and ordnance train needed for an advance upon Seringapatam. Feeling that the presence of the Governor-General would stimulate the local authorities to the exertions required to bring the campaign against

Tippoo Sultan to a successful issue, he induced his brother to transfer temporarily the headquarters of the Government of India from Fort William to Fort St. George.

The army of the Carnatic was assembled at Vellore early in 1799, and on February 11th it began its marches towards Seringapatam, being joined a week later by the Hyderabad subsidiary force under British officers, as well as a contingent of the Nizam's cavalry. The 33rd Foot was attached to this force, which numbered altogether about 16,000 men, and Colonel Wellesley was appointed to its command.

Simultaneously with the advance of the Madras army, a Bombay corps commanded by General Stuart was landed at Cannanore, and moved up the Western Ghauts to a point named Sedasir, where it was attacked by Tippoo. Tippoo was repulsed with some loss, and retired to the vicinity of Seringapatam, whence, after a short halt, he marched eastward for about twenty miles, and came into contact with General Harris's troops at Mellavelly. Being there defeated for the second time, he withdrew into Seringapatam, in front of which place he threw up a line of field intrenchments. General Harris resolved to make a night attack on these defences, and the operation was entrusted to Colonel Wellesley and

Colonel Shaw. The latter's attack was successful;
but owing to inadequate reconnaissance, as well as the
darkness of the night, and the thickness of the jungle,
Wellesley entirely failed in his object, and lost twelve

TIPPOO SULTAN.

grenadiers of the 33rd, whom Tippoo made prisoners
and tortured to death by causing nails to be hammered
into their skulls. The next morning, however, Tippoo's
intrenchments were carried without difficulty, and
shortly afterwards Seringapatam was invested by

General Harris, who meanwhile had been reinforced by General Stuart's column. On May 7th, 1799, the city was taken by assault, the command on this occasion being given to Major-General Baird, and the reserve in the trenches being placed in charge of Colonel Wellesley. The garrison fought with remarkable obstinacy, and in the course of the struggle Tippoo Sultan was killed in front of one of the city gates. The treasure captured in Seringapatam was valued at about £1,200,000 sterling, and Colonel Wellesley's share of it amounted to £7000 in money and £1200 in jewels. Two days after the assault, Colonel Wellesley was ordered to relieve General Baird as Governor of Seringapatam—a favour which, whether he owed it to his own merits, or to his being the brother of the Governor-General, was not unnaturally resented by the officer whom he superseded. After serving on a mixed commission appointed to report on the future government of Tippoo's dominions, Colonel Wellesley was invested with supreme civil and military control over the province and capital of Mysore, and in this capacity exhibited administrative abilities of a very high order. In May 1800, the Governor-General nominated Colonel Wellesley to the command of an expedition which it was proposed to send to Batavia with a view to inducing the Dutch to cede the

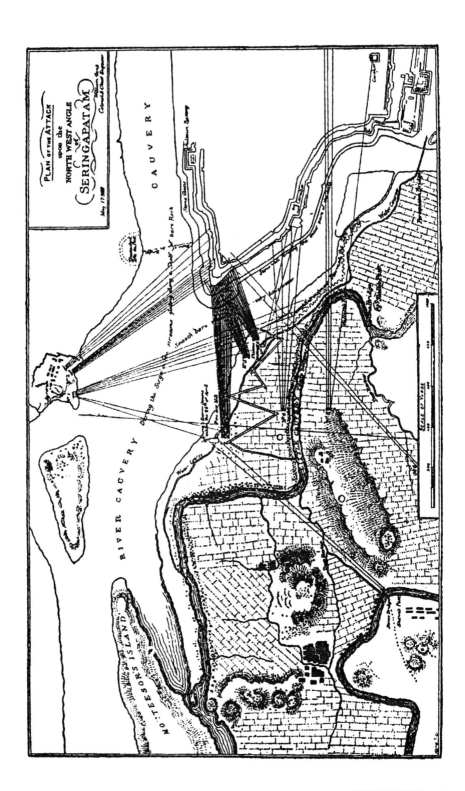

PLAN of the ATTACK upon the NORTH WEST ANGLE of SERINGAPATAM

island of Java to the English. This offer he declined
after consulting the Governor of Madras. His reason
for doing so was that he considered it a more important work to put a stop to the depredations of the
noted freebooter, Dhoondiah Waugh, who had been
seized and imprisoned by Tippoo, but regaining his
liberty on the fall of Seringapatam, had established
himself with a large following of about 40,000 men in
the Mahratta territory, between Goa and the western
frontier of Mysore. A British force was accordingly
assembled on the Tumbudra river, and the troops
being divided into three columns, a vigorous effort
was made to surround the band of marauders, and
capture its chief. After a series of long and rapid
marches through an arid and difficult country,
Wellesley came in contact with the main body of the
enemy at Manauli, a small fort about fifty miles east
of Belgaum, and after a cavalry skirmish pursued it
for a hundred and fifty miles to Konagull on the
Tumbudra, where, on September 10th, he again
attacked with his cavalry. This engagement was
decisive, Dhoondiah being killed, and his followers
completely broken up and dispersed.

Colonel Wellesley had declined the command of
the proposed expedition to Batavia when it was first
offered him, but on his return to Mysore after Dhoon-

diah Waugh had been disposed of, he received orders
to proceed to Trincomalee, where the force originally
intended for the annexation of Java was still being
collected.   At this period the attention of the Government, both at home and in India, was fixed on Egypt,
which had been occupied by the French with the
object of converting it into a base of operations against
the British possessions in the East.   The idea of
annexing Java had not been entirely abandoned, but
the Government of India was inclined to think that
it might be more advantageous either to capture
Mauritius, then a French colony, or to despatch an
Indian contingent to the Red Sea, where it might co-
operate with the force which was being prepared by
the home authorities for the purpose of driving the
French out of Egypt.   The question was decided by
the receipt of a despatch from His Majesty's Ministers,
ordering the Government of India to send 3000 men
to Egypt; and Wellesley, who on his arrival at Trincomalee was apprised of this order, at once arranged
on his own responsibility for the troops assembled at
that port to sail for Bombay, notwithstanding strong
remonstrance from the Governor of Ceylon.   When
called to account for acting in this matter without the
sanction of the Governor-General, Wellesley justified
himself on the ground that the movement from Trin-

comalee to Bombay would greatly expedite the arrival of the force at its ultimate destination, Bombay being the only port at which the requisite provisions and stores were obtainable, and where the transports could procure an adequate supply of fresh water before starting on the voyage to Kosseir in the Red Sea.

On reaching Bombay, Colonel Wellesley received the unwelcome news that the Government of India had appointed Major-General Baird to command the expedition, and that his own position would be that of second in command ; the Governor-General explaining to him in a very kind letter that the number of troops employed had rendered it necessary to appoint a general officer to the chief command, and giving him the option of returning to Mysore if he objected to serve under General Baird. Wellesley was bitterly disappointed at being, as he conceived, unfairly superseded, though the officer appointed to the command was much senior to himself, and he expressed his indignation in very forcible terms to his brother Henry. Still, he was disinclined to avail himself of the Governor-General's permission to return to Mysore, and he only did so because a severe attack of illness prevented him from accompanying the expedition.

On his recovery, in May 1801, Wellesley resumed

the government of Mysore, and for nearly two years occupied himself with the civil and military adminis-tration of that province.

In April 1802, at the age of thirty-three, and after fifteen years' service, he became a Major-General, his

LORD HARRIS.

promotion having been strongly urged upon His Royal Highness the Duke of York by his brother the Governor-General, who himself two years before had been raised to an Irish marquisate, with the title of the Marquis Wellesley.

About this time the evacuation of Egypt by the
French had relieved the Government of India from
the fear of external attack, and it seemed a fitting
opportunity to extend the influence of the East India
Company over the Mahratta confederacy, which at the
beginning of the century was extremely powerful, and,
if its members had acted in unison, might have
seriously endangered our ascendency in the East.
The nominal head of the confederacy was the Peshwa,
Bajee Rao, whose capital was Poona; its principal
members were Sindhia, Holkar, the Raja of Berar,
and the Gaekwar of Baroda. Of these Sindhia was
the most formidable, possessing a numerous army
with strong artillery and well-equipped cavalry. In a
semi-independent position, but still owing allegiance to
Sindhia, there was a force commanded by the French
adventurer Perron, numbering 30,000 infantry and
8000 cavalry, with 250 guns. This force, which was
to a great extent officered by Frenchmen, occupied
the important strongholds of Agra, Delhi, and Aligarh,
and dominated the rich country between the Jumna
and Ganges. The Raja of Berar was master of a
large extent of territory to the north of the Nizam's
dominions, stretching from Cuttack on the east to
Ellichpore on the west. Nagpore was the Raja's
capital, and his army consisted of about 20,000

disciplined cavalry and 10,000 infantry. Holkar's
possessions lay between those of Sindhia on the east
and the Bombay Presidency on the west. His army,
composed chiefly of cavalry, and, like Sindhia's, commanded by French officers, numbered about 80,000
men. Holkar and Sindhia, however, were extremely
jealous of each other; and the former, thinking that
the latter exercised undue influence at the Peshwa's
court, crossed the Nerbudda in 1802, marched upon
Poona, and defeated the combined forces of the Peshwa
and Sindhia. Bajee Rao fled from his capital and
sought refuge in British territory at Bassein, where he
threw himself upon the protection of the East India
Company. Taking advantage of this occurrence, the
Governor-General at the close of 1802 entered into
a treaty with the Peshwa, known as the treaty of
Bassein, which stipulated that the British Government
should reinstate Bajee Rao at Poona, and guard him
against the aggression of the rival Mahratta states,
while he on his part should be entirely guided in his
foreign policy by the Government of India, should
employ no Europeans hostile to the British, and should
assign territory sufficient to meet the cost of a subsidiary force similar to that maintained by the Nizam,
and exclusively commanded by British officers. The
Governor-General hoped to be able to carry this treaty

into effect without provoking the open hostility of the
Native States more or less directly concerned. The
provisions of the treaty, however, were so opposed to
the interests of the principal Mahratta chiefs, especially
those of Sindhia and the Raja of Berar, that Lord
Wellesley could not but recognise the strong probability
of their endeavouring by force or intrigue to recover
their ascendency at Poona, or to obtain compensation
in some other direction. To guard against such a con-
tingency, the Governor-General determined to mobilise
a portion of the army of each Presidency, and so to
distribute the troops at his disposal as to bring effective pressure to bear on the states likely to oppose
his policy. In November 1802 a force of 19,000 men,
drawn from the Madras army, was concentrated at
Hurryhur, on the north-west frontier of Mysore, and
shortly afterwards orders were given for a division
from Bombay, about 7000 strong, to be in readiness to
operate in the direction of Surat and Broach. A force
was collected at Calcutta for the occupation of the province of Cuttack ; and General Lake, the Commander-
in-Chief in India, was to be prepared to advance from
Cawnpore with 14,000 men against Perron's army holding Delhi, Agra, and the North-West Provinces. Three
reserve corps were also to be formed, for the purpose of
covering the possessions of the British and their Allies.

C

The first of these corps was to hold Poona and support the Peshwa's authority, the second was to take up a position on the river Kistna for the protection of the Nizam's territory, and the third was to be established at Mirzapore and Benares for the defence of the Ganges valley. Such a dissemination of force might under other circumstances have led to disaster, but, owing to the mutual jealousy of the Mahratta chiefs, combined action on their part was hardly to be apprehended, and the results of Lord Wellesley's bold and comprehensive scheme fully answered his expectations.

In February 1803 Major-General Wellesley, who was then at Seringapatam, received instructions to occupy Poona and reinstate Bajee Rao. Proceeding at once to Hurryhur, he assumed command of about 10,600 of the Madras troops assembled at that place ; and the Nizam's contingent numbering 8400 men, under Colonel Stevenson, was also placed under his orders, and directed to join him on the march. Leaving Hurryhur on March 9th, he effected a junction with Stevenson's troops on April 15th ; and three days later he received news that Amrat Rao, whom Holkar had entrusted with the Peshwa's authority on the latter escaping to Bassein, intended to burn Poona before retiring from that city on the approach of the British force. Wellesley determined, if possible, to save the city from destruction ; and, escorted by a cavalry detachment only 400 strong, he reached Poona by a forced march, in which he covered not less than sixty miles in thirty hours. Amrat Rao was taken by surprise and precipitately withdrew, after sending a submissive message to the British commander ; and Poona was occupied, without opposition, on April 20th. Bajee Rao was replaced on the *musnud* on May 13th, and the British force remained at his capital for some months, during which General Wellesley organised a pontoon train, repaired his ordnance carriages, provided depôts and magazines for the supply of his troops, and brought his transport and commissariat services into a thoroughly efficient state. In the meantime Holkar had retired to Indore, but Sindhia and the Raja of Berar had assumed a threatening attitude, and collected a large army at Burhanpur, on the river Taptee, near the Nizam's northern frontier. It became evident from the movement of their troops that, as soon as the rains were over and the rivers fordable, these Mahratta chiefs intended either to invade the Nizam's territory or to operate against the British in the direction of Poona. Towards the end of June the Governor-General conferred full military

and political powers on General Lake in Northern
India and on Major-General Wellesley in the Deccan,
and authorised them to take such action with regard
to Holkar, Sindhia, and the Berar Raja as might be
necessary to maintain the treaty of Bassein and to

GENERAL LAKE.

protect the rights and interests of the Government of
India and its Allies. Wellesley at once called upon
Sindhia and the Raja of Berar to prove their friendly
intentions by withdrawing their troops from Burhanpur to the stations where they were usually
quartered. He warned them that should they decline

to do so he would attack them ; and, as a preliminary to decisive action, he moved his force from Poona towards Ahmednagar, a fort and city at that time held by Sindhia. The Mahratta chiefs refused to withdraw unless the British force and the Nizam's contingent also retired to their ordinary cantonments. Wellesley accordingly declared war, and proceeded to attack Ahmednagar, which after a siege was captured, with slight loss, on the 11th August. The possession of this place greatly facilitated the offensive operations which Wellesley had in view, as it furnished an advanced base covering his main line of communication with Poona and Bombay, guarded the western portion of Hyderabad, and prevented the Mahratta chiefs from receiving any assistance from Southern India. Advancing from Ahmednagar on the 17th August Wellesley crossed the Godavery, and reached Aurungabad on the 24th of the same month ; and early in September Stevenson seized Jalna, an important fort on the Mahratta frontier.

On the 21st September Stevenson's force joined the main body, and arrangements were made to attack the united forces of Sindhia and the Raja of Berar on the 24th. Owing, however, to defective information as to the disposition of the enemy's troops, Wellesley ordered Stevenson to move by a different road from that taken by the force under his own immediate command, so that on the 23rd he alone encountered the Mahratta army strongly posted behind the river Kaitna, with its left supported by the village of Assaye and its front defended by 128 guns. The Mahrattas numbered 50,000, while Wellesley's force consisted of 1500 British and about 6500 Native soldiers, with only 17 guns. The troops, cavalry horses, and gun bullocks were greatly fatigued by a march of twenty-four miles ; but, after a rapid reconnaissance, Wellesley resolved on what he called "the desperate expedient" of at once attacking the enemy. The Mahrattas were drawn up in a long line with their infantry and artillery on the left and their cavalry on the right, a detachment of the latter being posted in front of the Kaitna in order to observe the movements of the British force. Wellesley decided to engage the left, and to do so he had to march along the enemy's front and to cross the Kaitna by a ford within easy range of the extreme left of the Mahratta position. On perceiving the object of this movement the French officers in command of the Mahratta infantry and artillery changed front with admirable precision, so as to bring their line parallel to that of the British infantry. The latter, after crossing the ford, was drawn up in two lines, supported in rear by the 19th Light Dragoons and the regular Native cavalry, and covered on its left flank by the Mysore and Peshwa's irregular cavalry. The General's intention was to push forward his left and thus penetrate the centre of the enemy's line. By some mistake, however, the officer commanding the piquets, which were upon the right, led immediately up to the village of Assaye, and this advance was followed by the 74th Foot in the second line, which had been ordered to support the piquets. The result was a serious break in both the infantry lines, and severe loss to the piquets and the 74th Regiment. Matters became so critical that the British and Native cavalry had to charge into the Mahratta batteries in order to extricate what was left of their infantry in this part of the field. On the left the 78th Foot and the Sepoy battalions advanced with the utmost gallantry, and, after firing only two rounds, engaged the enemy with the bayonet. The Mahratta infantry at last gave way, abandoning their guns, and our Sepoys pursued the fugitives up to the *nulla* or ravine which ran along the rear of the position. A number of Mahratta gunners sheltered themselves beneath their guns, and, as soon as the tide of battle had passed them, they rose up, and, turning their pieces round, began to fire on the rear of the British force. Wellesley averted this danger by placing himself at the head of the 78th Regiment and the 7th Native Cavalry, and, by a vigorous charge, again made himself master of the enemy's artillery. This final charge decided the fortune of the day : the Mahrattas broke, and fled in all directions : 1200 of the enemy were killed on the field of battle, and 800 more during the pursuit ; and 98 guns, with a large amount of ammunition and stores, were captured. Unfortunately the pursuit was not carried out so promptly and effectually as Wellesley desired, for our regular cavalry had lost its cohesion, owing to the necessity for employing it to extricate the piquets and the 74th Foot in their premature attack on the village of Assaye. On the British side the loss was extremely heavy, amounting in killed and wounded to 43 British officers, 540 non-commissioned officers and soldiers, 36 Native officers, and 1238 non-commissioned officers and soldiers.* Wellesley† himself

---

* Every officer of the 74th Highlanders present with the regiment was either killed or wounded, except Quartermaster James Grant, who, when he saw so many of his friends fall in the battle, resolved to share their fate, and, though a non-combatant, joined the ranks and fought to the termination of the action.

† Colin Campbell, brigade-major to General Wellesley, writing about Assaye, said : " The General was in the thick of the action the whole time, and had a horse killed under him. No

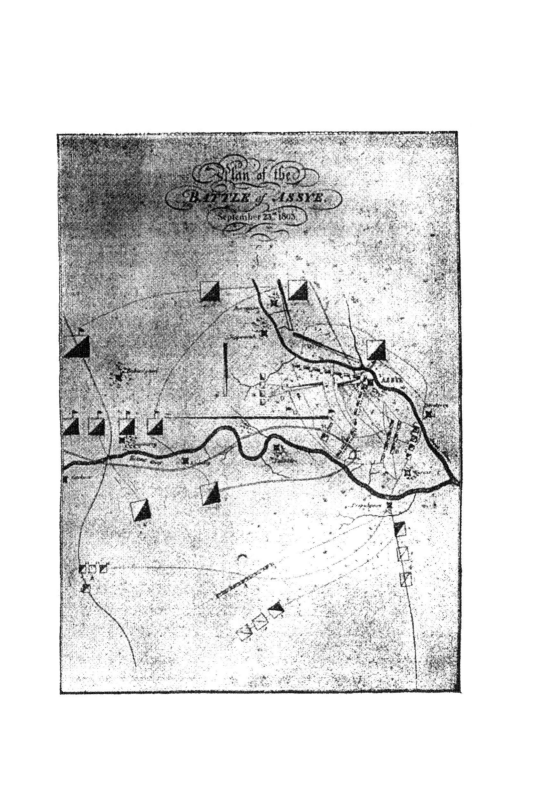

Plan of the
BATTLE of ASSYE.
September 23rd 1803.

had one horse shot and a second piked under him.
It was an infantry battle won almost entirely by the
use of the bayonet. The regular cavalry played a
secondary, but useful, part in the action, while the
irregular cavalry did little more than protect the left
flank from Sindhia's horsemen. The troops seriously
engaged were outnumbered by ten to one, and lost
more than a third of their total. The next day
Stevenson's force arrived in time to join in the
pursuit of the scattered Mahratta army, after which it
was ordered by Wellesley to march north of the
Taptee and lay siege to Burhanpur and Asirgarh ;
Wellesley himself undertaking to cover Stevenson
while thus employed, to protect the lines of communication, and to defend the frontiers of the Nizam
and the Peshwa. As a striking instance of Native
duplicity, it may be mentioned that both these chiefs,
who owed everything they possessed to the Government of India, did their utmost to thwart the operations of the British commander. The Nizam's officials
refused to accommodate our wounded in the fort of

---

man could have shown a better example to the troops than he
did. I never saw a man so cool and collected as he was,
though, I can assure you, till our troops got orders to advance,
the fate of the day seemed doubtful ; and, if the numerous
cavalry of the enemy had done their duty, I hardly think it
possible that we could have succeeded."

Dowlatabad ; and the conduct of the Peshwa was even more unfriendly, as he not only neglected to furnish the supplies which he had promised, but intrigued with Sindhia and the Raja of Berar against us.

While these events were taking place in the Deccan, equal activity had been displayed on our north-west frontier and in the neighbourhood of Cuttack. On the 7th August General Lake started from Cawnpore with 14,000 men, and after defeating Perron's troops before Aligarh, besieged and captured that stronghold. Perron thereupon signed an agreement not to fight again against the British, and was allowed to withdraw to Chandernagore, where he embarked for France, taking with him the enormous wealth which he had amassed in Sindhia's service. He was succeeded in command of Sindhia's troops by another Frenchman, named Bourquien, who retreated to a strong position covering Delhi, from which he was driven by General Lake with a loss of 68 guns and 3000 men, the British casualties being only 400 killed and wounded. Delhi fell into the conqueror's hands, and the Mogul emperor, Shah Alum, was replaced on the throne, and became a pensioner of the East India Company. Bourquien and the French officers serving under him made terms with General Lake, and were permitted to leave the country; and the Mahratta troops, thus deprived of their leaders, fell back on Agra, where, on the 10th October, they were again defeated and dispersed. The Agra garrison shortly afterwards surrendered, and the British force occupied the fort, which contained a large depôt of stores, 164 guns, and 28 lakhs of treasure. Sindhia, with surprising obstinacy, determined to continue the struggle, and formed a fresh corps about 16,000 strong with 70 guns, out of the remains of Perron's regiments, supplemented by fourteen of the best battalions of his own army. This corps was attacked by Lake at Laswarrie, near Agra, on the 1st November; 5000 of the Mahratta troops were killed or wounded; and the whole of Sindhia's guns, baggage, and stores fell into the hands of the British.

On the eastern side of the Peninsula the district of Cuttack, forming part of the Raja of Berar's territory, was occupied without much opposition by a column under Colonel Harcourt; and on the western side Colonel Woodington, acting under General Wellesley's orders, besieged the fort of Broach, which belonged to Sindhia, and took it by assault on the 29th August. Thus assailed on the north, south, and west, Sindhia endeavoured to gain time by proposing

an armistice, in which the Raja of Berar was not
included ; and this was agreed to early in November
by General Wellesley, who considered it would be advantageous to break up the alliance existing between
the two Mahratta chiefs and to continue the war against
the Raja of Berar. While negotiations were going on
between Wellesley and Sindhia, Colonel Stevenson
was directed to march from Asirgarh, which had
recently been captured, towards the Raja of Berar's
territory, and to lay siege to the fort of Gawilgarh.
Wellesley intended to cover and support Stevenson's
operations with his own force ; but on approaching
Gawilgarh he received information that Sindhia,
contrary to his agreement, had united his troops with
those of the Raja, and taken up a position threatening
the line of advance. Effecting a junction with
Stevenson's column, Wellesley moved in the direction
of the enemy, and on the 29th of November, after a
march of twenty-six miles, found the Mahratta army
drawn up in front of the village of Argaum.
Although it was late in the day, Wellesley decided
to attack, and drew up his troops in two lines,
the infantry in front, the regular cavalry in the second
line supporting the right, and the irregular cavalry
on the left. The British force numbered about 14,000,
exclusive of 4000 irregular horse ; and the Mahratta

force, consisting chiefly of cavalry, numbered 40,000.
When the first line came under the enemy's guns,
three of the Sepoy battalions which had behaved
with great gallantry at the battle of Assaye were
seized with a sudden panic and fled.   " Luckily," the
General remarked in a letter to his brother's military
secretary, " I happened to be at no great distance
from them, and I was able to rally them and re-
establish the battle.   If I had not been there, I am
convinced we should have lost the day."   This
incident necessitated the front line being reformed,
which caused some delay ; but eventually the infantry
advanced with great steadiness, the right being
pushed forward with the object of turning the
enemy's left.   On the failure of two attempts on the
part of the enemy's cavalry to throw the line into
confusion, which were repulsed with great slaughter,
the Mahrattas abandoned their position, leaving
38 guns with all their ammunition and stores on the
field.   The cavalry of the British force pursued the
enemy by moonlight for several miles, destroying
large numbers and capturing many elephants and
camels.   The total loss on the British side was not
very serious, amounting to 46 Europeans and Natives
killed and 293 wounded.

This victory having opened the road to Gawilgarh,

Wellesley ordered the troops under his immediate
command, together with Stevenson's column, to
resume their march on November 30th, and after a
short investment the fort was taken by assault on the
15th December, with a loss on the British side of only
126 killed and wounded. The governor of the fort,
his principal officers, and the greater part of the
garrison lost their lives ; and 52 guns, 2000 English
muskets, and a large quantity of ammunition fell
into the hands of the besiegers. These operations,
combined with the successes achieved in other parts
of India, resulted in the Raja of Berar and Sindhia
suing for peace ; and in December 1803 Wellesley
concluded treaties with them, under which they ceded
in perpetuity to the East India Company the
important cities of Delhi, Agra, Broach, and Ahmednagar, transferred territory yielding an annual
revenue of three millions sterling, and engaged not
to take any Europeans into their service except with
the sanction of the Government of India.

Early in 1804 Wellesley set out on his return
towards Poona, but on his way he found it necessary
to break up a band of Mahratta freebooters who had
been plundering along the western frontier of the
Nizam's dominions. Taking with him one British
and three Native cavalry regiments, and a small

detachment of infantry, he made a forced march of
sixty miles in thirty hours, and coming up with
the Mahratta force, already in retreat, he charged
it with his cavalry, and completely routed and dispersed it.

Wellesley visited Bombay on his way to Poona,
and from the latter place submitted an application to
the Commander-in-Chief in India for leave to return
to England on the ground of ill-health. He also
resigned the military and political powers vested in
him by the Governor-General. From Poona he was
ordered to Calcutta, which place he reached at the
beginning of August, by way of Seringapatam and
Madras. The following month the news arrived of
the reverses sustained by Colonel Monson, who had
been selected by General Lake to command a force
intended to drive Holkar out of Rajputana. Owing
to Monson's vacillation and incapacity, this force was
disastrously defeated, and Holkar's success seemed
likely to encourage Sindhia and the Raja of Berar to
renew their struggle against the British power. The
Governor-General offered his brother's services to
General Lake, but the latter preferred that Wellesley
should resume his previous command in the Deccan,
and accordingly he returned to Seringapatam at the
end of November. In December Holkar was de-

To face p. 32.

BATTLE OF ASSAYE.

feated by Lake, and all danger of a Mahratta combination was at an end.

In February, 1805, Wellesley again asked to be allowed to return to England, his health not having improved, and prolonged service in India being extremely distasteful to him. The Government and the military authorities raised no objection, and he embarked at Madras towards the end of March. Before leaving India he received news of his appointment to be an extra Knight Companion of the Bath, which, under the original constitution of the order, was a higher distinction than the Grand Cross of the Bath is at present, and the thanks of the King and Parliament were communicated to him in a general order by the Governor-General in Council.

There can, I think, be little doubt that much of Wellington's subsequent success in the Peninsula was due to the experience he gained in India as a soldier, a politician, and an administrator. The dunce of the family, the somewhat frivolous aide-de-camp to the Lord-Lieutenant of Ireland, the young man whom his mother considered to be only food for powder, was able to show in the retreat from Antwerp to Bremen that he knew how to manœuvre his battalion and to command a rear-guard. On his arrival in India he

D

found himself in a country where in almost every matter the power and influence of the Governor-General were supreme, and the Governor-General being his brother, he was quickly placed in a position of responsibility, which gave him the opportunity of developing his talents as a soldier and statesman in the best of all schools—the school of practice. It cannot be denied that in early life Wellington owed much to family influence, and to a system of promotion which would now be stigmatised as jobbery. On the other hand, he took full advantage of every chance that was thrown in his way, and by his industry and capacity fully justified the exceptional favour with which he was treated.

The following appear to me to be the most interesting points in Wellington's early career. First, the hardships suffered by the British soldiers in the retreat through Holland seem to have impressed upon him the necessity for keeping troops employed on field service in the best possible fighting condition, and his views on this point were strengthened by what he observed and learned in India, the result being that no commander has ever realised more fully than he did that the efficiency of a field army can only be maintained by attending most carefully and constantly to the organisation of its several depart-

ments. When the force was being prepared at
Madras and Vellore for the siege of Seringapatam,
Wellesley himself supervised the commissariat and
transport arrangements. Later, when he was entrusted with an independent command, his first
thought was to improve his bullock train; and in
order to supplement his departmental resources he encouraged the Brinjarries, or itinerant grain merchants,
to attach themselves to his force by promising them
protection and liberal treatment. He took every
precaution to ensure the safety of his convoys, and
gave the most minute instructions for the periodical
replenishment of his supply depôts. He spared
neither time nor trouble in dealing with such matters
as the repair of his ordnance carriages and the
provision of a pontoon train. Finding when he
occupied Poona that serious delay was likely to occur
in procuring new gun wheels from Bombay, he
established workshops of his own, and he drew up an
elaborate memorandum on the subject of pontoons,
in which he not only gave the dimensions of the
requisite boats and equipment, but described in detail
the method of laying a bridge. He was strongly
averse to the system of requisitions, as being almost
certain to demoralise the troops and alienate the
population of the country. He always endeavoured,

therefore, to obtain supplies either by transporting
them from his advanced depôts, by purchase on the
spot, or through the agency of the Brinjarries.
Indian campaigns of a century ago resemble in their
main features those which have been carried on in
later years on the borders of our Indian Empire. It
is one of the peculiarities of Asiatic warfare that
the facilities and resources which are furnished by
European civilisation for the concentration, movement, and subsistence of large bodies of men are
either entirely wanting, or exist in such a rudimentary
form that considerable skill and practical experience
are required to turn them to the best account. A
commander of troops in India cannot hope to be
successful unless he has acquainted himself with every
detail of his profession. He must know not only how
to manœuvre and fight, but how to feed and clothe
his men, to arrange for their payment, to provide for
the care of the sick and wounded, and to improvise
the means for overcoming the countless difficulties
which are continually presenting themselves in the
course of a campaign. From the time of Clive up to
the present day India has been a valuable training
school for the British army, and to none were its
lessons of greater advantage than to the illustrious
soldier who in the Peninsula and the Netherlands

adhered to the principles and methods which he had learnt in the East.

The rapid development of Wellington's administrative talents is in the highest degree remarkable. Placed, at the age of thirty, at the head of the civil and military government of Mysore, he quickly restored order throughout that conquered province, and though, in his opinion, the natives of India, both Hindus and Mohammedans, were incurably vicious, cruel, and deceitful, he acted towards them with such fairness and liberality that they accepted his rule as a welcome change from the tyranny of their own princes. He displayed the same equitable and indulgent spirit in his dealings with the Nizam and the Mahratta chiefs, and it was mainly owing to the confidence which he inspired in the minds of Sindhia and the Raja of Berar that he was able to conclude treaties with them so advantageous to the East India Company. He had to be constantly on his guard against the treachery and duplicity of the Native rulers, who, while nominally the Allies of the British Government, did their utmost to defeat his plans and embarrass his movements. Nevertheless he uniformly acted in the most conciliatory manner towards them, and by maintaining the strictest order and discipline among the troops under his command, did all in his power for the protection of the life and property of the people of the country. He thus established British prestige and the influence of the British Government throughout the Deccan and Southern India.

Another point deserving of notice is Wellington's correct appreciation of our position as an alien Power controlling a vast and heterogeneous Oriental population. He pointed out, in words as true now as when they were written, that the Government of India depends for its stability on the sword, and that, as our responsibilities become greater with the extension of our territory, the cost of the army must proportionately increase. To use his own words, "the conclusion of the most successful foreign war in India, that by which the most formidable enemy may have been subdued, if it gives an accession of territory, must bring with the territory a necessity to increase the army, because the government must be established in the new territory, and supported, as well as in the old, by the power of the sword. The want of knowledge, or rather of recollection of these facts, is the cause of all the complaints of high military establishments and expenses." Is not this the case at the present time? A cry is being raised against the cost of the army in India, in forgetfulness of the fact that

Baluchistan and Upper Burma have within the last fifteen years been added to the Empire, and that the rapid advance of a rival Power has obliged us to strengthen and improve our army, and to spend money on the necessary defence of the North-West Frontier. It seems also to be forgotten that the revenue of India is collected in rupees, while many of the charges for the army have to be paid in sterling.

With respect to the distribution of the army in India, Wellington was at first in favour of keeping the greater portion of the troops in standing camps, and of holding only those fortresses which appeared to be indispensable to the internal security of the country. Before he left India he changed his views, and recommended that most of the existing forts should be kept up, and that the troops in each province should be concentrated in a few healthy and well-situated cantonments, with their field equipage always in readiness. This arrangement, he thought, would increase the mobility of the troops, and would admit of their discipline and training, as well as their health, being more carefully attended to. Of the soundness of this principle there can be no doubt, but for many years after Wellington's departure from India an opposite course was followed, until the disasters of the Mutiny impressed upon the Government and the military authorities the advantages of concentration.

It is also worthy of note that Wellington was strongly in favour of encouraging the Native States to keep up armies capable of taking the field and assisting in the defence of the country. This policy, I am glad to say, has lately been accepted by the Government of India, and the Imperial Service contingents maintained by the principal feudatories of the Empire will, if judiciously managed, add very materially to our military strength.

As regards the knowledge of strategy and tactics displayed by Wellington in the course of his field operations, it is evident that he fully realised the supreme importance in Eastern warfare of promptitude of action, and audacity in assuming the offensive even though the enemy might be enormously superior in number. This was shown at the battle of Assaye, where, if he had hesitated in the smallest degree, a serious defeat, instead of a brilliant victory, would have been the result. On that occasion his dispositions are certainly open to criticism. His knowledge of the enemy's movements was so defective that he came upon the Mahratta army a day sooner than he expected, and before he had been joined by the large portion of his force which was

under Colonel Stevenson's command. Having, however, resolved to attack, he marched his troops along
the enemy's front in the immediate presence of a
large body of hostile cavalry ; and the ford by which
he crossed the Kaitna was not only under the fire of
the Mahratta artillery, but capable of being easily
defended by a detachment of the Mahratta infantry.
"Luckily," he wrote, "they did not occupy the ford.
If they had, I must have gone lower down ; and
possibly I should have been obliged to make a road
across the river, which would have taken so much
time that I should not have had day enough to
attack." When the river had been crossed the
premature advance of the right of his line threw the
infantry on that flank into confusion, and to relieve it
he had to make use of his cavalry, which consequently
lost its cohesion and was unable to make a vigorous
pursuit.

At the battle of Argaum the arrangements were
more carefully matured, the entire British force was
united, and the enemy, dispirited by a previous defeat,
did not offer the same stubborn resistance as at
Assaye. Here again Wellington's promptitude and
decision were displayed, for he engaged the enemy at
once, though his troops were fatigued by a long
march and it was late in the day before the attack

could be delivered. So with the sieges of Ahmednagar, Burhanpur, Asirgarh, and Gawilgarh ; they
were conducted with skill and foresight, and the
general plan of campaign was admirably designed to
protect the Allies of the East India Company, to drive
the Mahrattas out of the Deccan, and to break up the
alliance between Sindhia and the Raja of Berar.

The first three volumes of "Wellington's Dis-
patches," which relate to India, throw considerable
light on his personal character. He seems to have
been an ambitious man, with a high opinion of his
own qualifications and services. He had no fear of
responsibility, and whatever duty was entrusted to
him he desired to carry it out free from all interference
or control on the part of equal or superior authority.
There is no doubt he rendered most valuable
assistance to the Commander-in-Chief of the Madras
army in supervising the transport and commissariat
arrangements previous to the advance on Seringapatam ; and it appears that General Harris not only
treated him with friendship and confidence, but also
brought his services to the special notice of his brother
the Governor-General. Still he complained to the
latter that the Commander-in-Chief adopted his ideas
without giving him due credit for them, and remarked :
" I wish for several reasons that you had a com-

mander-in-chief under you who, when he approved of the conduct of an officer, would have a sufficiency of spirit to make known his approbation." When Seringapatam had been captured, and Wellesley was appointed Commandant of that city in supersession of Major-General Baird, he does not seem to have

MAJOR-GENERAL BAIRD.

realised that the latter officer had been hardly treated, or that he himself owed his exceptional advancement to his relationship with the Governor-General. When he was made military and civil Governor of the province of Mysore, it had at first been intended to associate with him a civil commissioner, who had been attached to the Nizam's contingent during the campaign. Wellington refused point blank to divide his authority with any one, expressing himself to the Marquis Wellesley in the following forcible terms: " I intend to ask to be brought away with the army if any civil servant of the Company is to be here, or any person with civil authority who is not under my orders ; for I know that the whole is a system of job and corruption from beginning to end, of which I and my troops would be made the instruments." Then followed his mortification at finding that the Government of India had thought proper to appoint a Major-General to command the expedition to Egypt, and his annoyance at the selection of General Baird. On this occasion he wrote to his brother Henry : " This supersession has ruined all my prospects, founded upon any service that I may have rendered. . . . It must have been occasioned either by my own misconduct, or by an alteration in the sentiments of the Governor- General. I have not been guilty of robbery or murder, and he has certainly changed his mind ; but the world, which is always good-natured towards those whose affairs do not exactly prosper, will not, or rather does not, fail to suspect that both, or worse, have been the occasion of my being banished, like General Kray, to my estate in Hungary." Just before

Wellington left India he wrote very bitterly about the East India Company : " I have served the Company in important situations for many years, and have never received anything but injury from the Court of Directors." There is, however, nothing to show in what particular way he had suffered at the hands of these gentlemen.

The failure of Wellington's health was, no doubt, one of his principal reasons for deciding to return to England. At the same time he had come to the conclusion that it was opposed to his own interests to stay longer in India, as he felt convinced that his services in that country, however distinguished they might be, would give him no claim to advancement in the home army. " I think," he says, " that I have served as long in India as any man ought, who can serve anywhere else ; and I think that there appears a prospect of service in Europe, in which I should be more likely to get forward." And again—" I acknowledge that I never have been very sanguine in my expectations that military services in India would be considered in the scale in which are considered similar services in other parts of the world."

It is pleasant to notice that, during his stay in India, Wellington, though extremely strict in matters of discipline, was kind and considerate to the troops under his command, and was respected and liked by his officers. Mr. Gleig, in his Life of Wellington, quotes the following passage from a letter written in 1802 by a young officer of the East India Company's Service to his friends in England : " Everything goes well, because Colonel Wellesley is in command. Whatever he undertakes he does admirably. Perhaps it was hardly fair to employ him rather than General —— ; but we are all delighted to have him at our head, he makes us so confident and so comfortable." Major-General Nicolls refers in his journal to the attention paid by Wellington to the sick and wounded after the battle of Assaye. He furnished them with wine from his own stock, repeatedly visited them, and made every possible arrangement for their comfort. He regarded it as most important from a financial and military, as well as from a humanitarian point of view, that proper care should be taken of the health of the British soldier in India. Writing to Colonel Murray on the subject of the barracks at Surat, he observed : "Every attention must be paid to economy, but I consider nothing in this country so valuable as the life and health of the British soldier, and nothing so expensive as soldiers in hospital. I request you to pay particular attention to their discipline and regularity, and to prevent their getting intoxicating liquors, which tend to their destruction." Wellington's appreciation of the good qualities of our Native soldiers is shown by his repeatedly comparing them in after life to the Portuguese troops, who, towards the close of the Peninsular War, attained a very high standard of efficiency. "The Sepoys," he used to say, "like the Portuguese, would go anywhere and do anything, when led by British officers and supported by British troops."

So highly was Wellington esteemed in the army of the Deccan, that, when he relinquished his command, the officers who had served under his immediate orders presented him with a service of plate of the value of two thousand guineas.

There are many other points of interest in Wellington's Indian career, with which I am unable to deal within the limits of this article. His indefatigable industry, his sound and cool judgment, and his political sagacity were as remarkable as his military talents. A masterful, ambitious man, he went home apparently somewhat disappointed with the results of his eight years' service in the East, and determined to push his way in a wider field than India afforded. Yet during those eight years he had risen to the rank of Major-General and become a K.B., had acquired a large amount of prize money at Seringapatam and in the Deccan, had been entrusted with high military command, and had filled important administrative and political appointments. His return to England was opportune. His country needed the services of an officer who to the vigour and audacity of youth united a sound judgment, an equable temper, and a thorough knowledge of his profession. His opportunity was not long in coming, and "the Sepoy General," as he was contemptuously styled by those who underrated the value of an Indian training, was soon to show the nations of Europe that he could be a match, and more than a match, for the Marshals of France.

"In the beginning of each war England has to seek
in blood the knowledge necessary to ensure success;
and, like the fiend's progress toward Eden, her con-
quering course is through chaos followed by death."—
NAPIER, 'Peninsular War.'

CHAPTER II.

As stated in my previous chapter, Major-General Sir
Arthur Wellesley, K.B., left India in March 1805,
and, after an absence of nine years, reached England
in September. Shortly after his arrival, he was
selected for the command of a brigade in an expedition to Hanover under Lord Cathcart. But the
victory which Napoleon gained at Austerlitz in
December broke up the European coalition against
him, and the British troops had hardly landed in
Germany before it was found necessary to recall
them. On the return of the expedition, in February
1806, Major-General Wellesley was appointed to
command an infantry brigade at Hastings, and soon
afterwards was elected Member of Parliament for

E

Rye. He took an active part in the House of Commons in defending his brother's administration as
Governor-General of India, which had been impugned
by a party opposed to the territorial aggrandisement
of the East India Company. General Wellesley's
clear exposition of the nature of our rule in India
and of the perils which had been avoided by the
adoption of a resolute course of action in dealing with
the Mahratta States, convinced a large majority of the
House of Commons, and a vote was passed in support
of his brother's policy.

In September 1806 the death of Fox led to the
formation of a new Ministry, with the Duke of Portland at its head. The Duke of Richmond was
appointed Lord-Lieutenant of Ireland, and in April
1807 Major-General Wellesley accepted the office of
Chief Secretary for that country. During the early
part of the same year the victories of Eylau and
Friedland made Napoleon absolute master on the
Continent, and induced the Emperor of Russia to
enter into an alliance with the French, the terms
of which were ostensibly embodied in the treaty of
Tilsit. In connection with this treaty, however, there
were certain secret articles, one of them being that
the Danish fleet should be placed at Napoleon's
disposal. This arrangement seriously menaced the

sea power of England, and the British Government determined to despatch a combined naval and military expedition to Copenhagen for the purpose of seizing the Danish ships, dockyard, and arsenal. The troops ordered on this service, numbering 27,000 men, were commanded by Lord Cathcart; the reserve, consisting of four infantry battalions with some German horse, being placed under Major-General Wellesley.

The object of the expedition was kept a profound secret until the force had arrived at its destination, when Lord Cathcart called upon the Danish Government to place its fleet and maritime stores in the temporary custody of England, pending the conclusion of a general European peace. The Prince Royal of Denmark refused to accede to this summons, and endeavoured by all the means in his power to prevent its enforcement. Lord Cathcart, therefore, invested the city, and directed General Wellesley with a division about 5000 strong to attack and disperse the Danish troops operating in the field. Wellesley found the latter, to the number of about 14,000, occupying a position at Kioge, the front of which was protected by earthworks; and after a short engagement defeated them with considerable loss. Meanwhile, batteries had been constructed by the investing army; and, after being bombarded for three days by these

E 2

batteries, and by the guns of the British fleet, Copenhagen capitulated, and the demands of the British
Government were complied with.   England thus obtained possession of fifteen line-of-battle ships, several
frigates, and 20,000 tons of naval stores.   The action
taken by the Cabinet was not only prompt and
decisive, but also somewhat unusual, if judged by the
ordinary rules of international comity.   On this account
it has been condemned by many Continental writers.
Nevertheless, the course adopted appears to have
been justifiable, on the ground that Napoleon's secret
compact with Russia threatened our maritime supremacy—and consequently, our national existence—
by handing over to the French Emperor the resources
of a neutral state, which, however well disposed
towards us, was too weak to preserve its neutrality.
General Wellesley distinguished himself in Zealand,
not only by his defeat of the Danish troops at Kioge,
but by the strict discipline which he maintained among
his own men, and the protection which he afforded to
the inhabitants of the island.

The expedition returned to England in October,
General Wellesley preceding it by a few weeks in
order to resume his functions as Secretary for Ireland.
In February 1808, he received the thanks of Parliament for his conduct at Copenhagen, and in the July

following, he was appointed to command an expedition which was being assembled at Cork for operations in Portugal or the south of Spain.

Before describing Wellington's campaign in the Peninsula, it seems desirable briefly to refer to the condition of affairs then prevailing in that part of Europe. After the conclusion of the treaty of Tilsit, Napoleon had, for the time, disposed of all his Continental enemies, and, at the instigation of Russia, he resolved first to subjugate Portugal, and afterwards to expel the Bourbon dynasty from Spain, substituting his brother Joseph for Charles IV. Russia encouraged the French Emperor in his designs upon the Peninsula, first, in order to withdraw his attention from Poland, and, secondly, in the event of a general peace, to secure his assent to the incorporation in the Russian Empire of Finland, Wallachia, and Moldavia. Napoleon was anxious to completely subjugate Portugal, because that country was the traditional ally of England, and an extensive and lucrative trade was carried on between the two nations. He also regarded it as necessary to his Continental system, and conducive to the strength and permanence of his dynasty, that a member of his own family should replace the Bourbons on the Spanish throne. The Portuguese as a race were well disposed towards England, and ready to welcome

British assistance in maintaining their independence. The Spaniards, on the other hand, wished to be left alone to manage their own affairs ; and though they objected to French interference, and greedily accepted the money and stores which the British

SIR HEW DALRYMPLE.

Government so lavishly supplied, they appear to have disliked the English even more than they did the French. This is shown by the speech which Castaños made to the French officers after the affair at Baylen, when he remarked : "Let not Napoleon persevere in aiming at a conquest which is unattainable.

Let him not force us into the arms of the English. They are hateful to us, and up to the present moment we have rejected their proffered succours." The revolt of the Spanish colonies in America increased the ill-feeling against England. This revolt was as ruinous to Spain as it was advantageous to our own merchants, who were enabled to participate in a transatlantic trade which had previously been monopolised by the parent kingdom.

As regards the Portuguese and Spanish troops, both at first were equally useless, not on account of the inferiority of the raw material, but because the officers were bigoted, conceited, and devoid of any idea of discipline and subordination. The Portuguese, however, were wise enough to recognise their own inefficiency, and to submit themselves to the control of British officers, under whose supervision they gradually improved until, in Wellington's opinion, they became equal to the native troops of the East India Company. The Spaniards, a manly and martial race, with glorious military traditions, could neither learn nor forget. They would not tolerate for a moment the interference of any foreign agency with the discipline and organisation of their soldiers. "I am quite convinced," said Wellington, "that the Spanish officers would rather submit to France than consent to give to us the smallest authority over their troops ; neither will they allow that our officers know more than their own." And yet these troops were so badly commanded as to be almost worthless. Wellington remarked of them : " They are mere children in the art of war : they know only how to advance, how to take to flight, and reassemble again, as if they were in a state of nature." One of their own generals, the Duke of Albuquerque, speaking of Cuesta's army, made the following admission : " In our marches we stopped to rest like a flock of sheep, without taking up any position. By-and-by we resumed our journey like pilgrims, without paying any attention to distances, order, or formation." Napoleon was of a similar opinion. Writing in August 1808, he said : " The whole body of insurrectionary forces is incapable of beating 25,000 French in a good position." And Berthier, in a letter to Joseph Bonaparte, dated January 31st, 1810, observed : " The Emperor considers that the English alone are formidable in Spain. The rest are the merest *canaille*, which can never keep the field."

Another obstacle to the proper organisation of the national forces for the defence of the Peninsula was the violent animosity that existed between the Spaniards and Portuguese—an animosity of long standing, which had been fostered by the convention entered into by Napoleon and Charles IV. in 1807, providing for the expulsion from Portugal of the reigning house of Braganza, and the partition of that country and its colonial possessions between France and Spain.

Yet another difficulty was the state of official and popular feeling in England. The British Government had but little confidence in the capacity of its military commanders. Pitt, as Lord Rosebery points out in his Life of that statesman, "had no generals. He discovered the genius of Wellington, but did not live to profit by it." Previously, when Lord North had a list of officers submitted to him for the commands in America, he observed : "I know not what effect these names may have on the enemy, but I know they make me tremble." "It was doubted," says Lord Londonderry, "whether among our own generals there could be found any capable of opposing the experienced and skilful warriors of France. We had never been accustomed to carry on war upon a large scale except in India ; and in India it was believed, for the successful conduct of a campaign, talents of the first order were hardly required." On the other hand the British public attached undue value to the national spirit and patriotism of the Spaniards. They imagined that enthusiasm could take the place of

dicipline and training, and when they saw Spain over-
run, and the Spanish fortresses and capital occupied
by French troops, they were inclined to blame their
own officers rather than the arrogance and imbecility
of those responsible for the organisation of the Spanish
army. From the foregoing remarks it will be seen
that, in attempting to maintain the independence of
the Peninsula, the British Government was undertaking a task of extraordinary difficulty, and that a
successful issue could not be hoped for unless our
operations against the French were directed by a
commander possessing military, diplomatic, and
administrative talents of quite an exceptional order.
Fortunately for England and Europe, such a man
was forthcoming in the person of Wellington.

In the summer of 1807 Napoleon sent a force under
Junot to invade Portugal and occupy Lisbon. Shortly
afterwards the principal Spanish fortresses were seized
by the French, and an army under Murat's command
captured Madrid in March 1808. Two months later
Charles IV. ceded his throne to the French Emperor,
who nominated his brother Joseph to succeed the
Bourbon king. Joseph entered his capital in July,
but had not been there many days before the Spanish
nation rose in revolt, attacked the French troops, and
forced their new sovereign to retire behind the Ebro.

The British Ministry assisted the Spaniards with large supplies of money and warlike stores, and in July 1808 determined to send an expedition to the Tagus with the object of expelling the French from Portugal and inducing the inhabitants of that country

LIEUTENANT-GENERAL THE HON. JOHN HOPE.

to join in the insurrection against Napoleon. The expeditionary force at first numbered about 9500 men, and the command of it was given to Wellesley, who in April 1808 had been promoted to the rank of Lieutenant-General. General Wellesley received his instructions from Lord Castlereagh on June 30th.

A fortnight later the Cabinet thought it desirable to raise the force to a strength of 30,000 men, and to appoint Sir Hew Dalrymple to the chief command, with Sir H. Burrard as second in command. Under this new arrangement Lieutenant-General Wellesley was to command one of the four divisions of the army, the other divisional commanders being Lieutenant-Generals the Hon. J. Hope, Lord Paget, and Mackenzie Fraser. General Wellesley sailed from Cork early in July, and after touching at Coruña in order to ascertain the state of affairs in Northern Spain, resolved to disembark his troops at Mondego Bay, in preference to the mouth of the Tagus, which was defended by forts held by French soldiers and by Russian men-of-war. Major-General Spencer, who was commanding a corps about 4800 strong at Cadiz, was ordered to join General Wellesley, and fortunately arrived at Mondego Bay about the same time as the convoy from Cork. The French troops at Junot's disposal did not exceed 20,000 men, and of these not more than 17,000 were available for the defence of Lisbon. One of his divisions, under General Loison, was posted at Estremoz, on the Spanish frontier. This he recalled by the Abrantes road, and sent Laborde from Lisbon to check the British advance and effect a junction with Loison at

Leiria. General Wellesley, whose force, including the reinforcement from Cadiz, numbered less than 14,000, and was especially weak in cavalry and artillery, moved rapidly southward, forestalled Laborde in the occupation of Leiria, and compelled him to retire upon Roliça, a village covering the road to Torres Vedras. Laborde was thus prevented from joining Loison, whose division had only just reached Santarem. On August 17th Wellesley attacked Laborde at Roliça, and, after a severe engagement, in which the British lost 420 killed and wounded and the French 600, drove him back towards Torres Vedras. The next day the British commander did not follow up the enemy, first, because his cavalry numbered only 470 sabres, and secondly, because he had received news of the arrival of two additional brigades from home, and thought it advisable to take up a position near Vimeiro to cover their landing. This operation occupied two days, and during the interval Junot was able to bring up Loison's division, and to concentrate and reorganise his troops at Torres Vedras. Marching thence on the evening of August 20th, he attacked early next morning the position held by the British at Vimeiro. It had been Wellesley's intention to assume the offensive and to cut off the enemy from their base by a flank march

along the sea coast, but the proposal was negatived
by Sir H. Burrard, who reached Maceira Bay on the
20th. but did not disembark until the following
morning.   The result of the engagement at Vimeiro
was entirely in favour of the British force.   The
French lost 1800 killed and wounded, and thirteen
guns, while the casualties on the English side did not
exceed 720.   General Burrard appeared on the field
of battle, but did not interfere with the dispositions
of his predecessor in command, except to halt one of
the brigades at a most inopportune moment.   By
noon the fate of the day was decided, and Wellesley
proposed at once to push forward with five brigades
with the object of forcing Junot into the Tagus valley,
while three other brigades, penetrating the defiles of
Torres Vedras, might occupy Mafra and cut off the
French from Lisbon.   Burrard hesitated, consulted
his subordinates, and decided not to move.   This
resolve so annoyed Wellesley that he remarked to
his staff : " Gentlemen, there is nothing for us to do
now but to hunt red-legged partridges."   Burrard's
excessive caution enabled Junot to regain, on the
evening of the 21st, the position at Torres Vedras
which he had previously occupied, and the next day
Sir Hew Dalrymple landed and assumed the chief
command.   He also was in doubt whether to await

reinforcements or to order an immediate advance, when the question was settled for him by Junot, who proposed an armistice and subsequently opened negotiations for the evacuation of Portugal by the French army. General Wellesley was present as an assessor when the terms of the armistice were being discussed between the French General Kellermann and Sir Hew Dalrymple ; and although he considered that the conditions acceded to by the British commander were unduly favourable to the enemy, he signed the preliminary memorandum, dated August 22nd, at the request of General Dalrymple, who regarded it as derogatory to his own dignity as a commander-in-chief to treat directly with an officer of inferior rank. The final convention was negotiated by the Quartermaster-General of the force, Colonel George Murray, and signed by him and General Kellermann on August 30th.

Writing on September 6th to the Bishop of Oporto, General Wellesley remarked : " Sir Hew Dalrymple, the present Commander-in-Chief, landed on the morning of August 22nd ; and on that evening he negotiated in person with the French General Kellermann an agreement of the suspension of hostilities. I was present during the negotiation of this agreement ; and, by the desire of the Commander-in-Chief,

I signed it. But I did not negotiate it, nor can I in any manner be considered responsible for its contents." A week before he had written privately to Lord Castlereagh, informing him that matters were not prospering, and that he wished to leave the army. He added: "I have been too successful with this army ever to serve with it in a subordinate situation, with satisfaction to the person who shall command it, and of course not to myself." On September 5th he again addressed Lord Castlereagh in the following terms: "It is quite impossible for me to continue any longer with this army; and I wish, therefore, that you would allow me to return home and resume the duties of my office; or, if not, that I should remain upon the staff in England; or, if that should not be practicable, that I should remain without employment." Sir Hew Dalrymple was equally disinclined to retain General Wellesley's services, and conveyed to him Lord Castlereagh's proposal that he should be sent to examine the northern provinces of Spain and report on the possibility of defending them against a French invasion. Wellesley declined this mission, pointing out to Sir Hew Dalrymple that he was not a topographical engineer, and could not pretend to describe in writing such a country as the Asturias. Sir Hew Dalrymple apparently accepted this as a valid excuse, for he suggested that officers of the Quartermaster-General's department might more fittingly be employed on such a duty.

General Wellesley was eventually permitted to leave the army, and he reached London on October 6th. Before his departure the general officers who had served under him while he was directing the operations presented him with a piece of plate, of the value of a thousand guineas, as a testimony of their high esteem and respect, and of their satisfaction at having had the good fortune to serve under his command.

On Wellesley's return home a great outcry was raised against the convention of Cintra, and the public were inclined to throw the blame on him, rather than on Sir Hew Dalrymple, who was really responsible. The Government, however, recalled Sir Hew and his second in command, and assembled a court of inquiry, which arrived at no specific conclusion on the subject of the armistice and convention, merely advising that no further proceedings should be taken, and declaring that unquestionable zeal and firmness had been displayed by Generals Dalrymple, Burrard, and Wellesley. The popular indignation having by this means been pacified, the thanks of Parliament for the victory of Vimeiro were accorded to General Wellesley in January 1809.

E

In the meantime the chief command of the British army in Portugal had devolved on Sir John Moore, who was feebly supported by the home authorities, and much hampered by the ill-advised interference of Mr. Frere, the British Minister at the headquarters of the provisional Spanish Government. In November 1808 Napoleon, after confirming his alliance with Russia and obtaining the Tzar's recognition of Joseph as King of Spain, proceeded to Vittoria to assume the command of the French forces in the Peninsula. He there issued a proclamation to his soldiers, promising them an easy victory over the British army, and assuring them that " le hideux léopard qui souille la Péninsule de sa présence prendra honteusement la fuite à notre aspect." The French Emperor rapidly overthrew the Spanish levies, and occupied Madrid on December 4th. Here he received intelligence that Sir John Moore was advancing into the north of Spain to the relief of the capital, and at once concentrated an overwhelming force for the purpose of cutting off the British army from the Tagus and the Galician ports. Moore had reluctantly committed himself to an offensive movement in answer to the earnest appeal of the Junta and Mr. Frere, and he naturally relied on the co-operation of the Spanish troops and civil authorities. Receiving, however, no

support either in men or in supplies, he found himself
in an extremely perilous position, and was obliged to
withdraw as rapidly as possible.   In spite of innumerable difficulties, he conducted his retreat in a most
masterly manner ; and after reaching Coruña, on
January 12th, 1809, defeated the enemy on the 16th,

COLONEL GEORGE MURRAY.

and died a hero's death on the field of battle.   The
British troops embarked the next day unmolested by
the French, and Marshal Soult, who was in command
of the latter, caused a monument to be erected in his
opponent's honour.   Moore's reputation has been
unjustly assailed.   He was one of the ablest and

most progressive of British generals ; but, in common
with most of his countrymen, he made the mistake of
supposing that the undisciplined Spanish forces could
offer an effective resistance to the veteran soldiers of
France.   This belief appears to have been shared at
the time by Wellington, who, in a letter to the Hon.
C. Stewart, dated September 1st, 1808, referred to
Sir Hew Dalrymple's inaction in the following words :
" I do not know what Sir Hew Dalrymple proposes
to do, or is instructed to do ; but, if I were in his
situation, I would have twenty thousand men at
Madrid in less than a month from this time."

In the spring of 1809 the general state of affairs
was as follows.   The British Ministry was perplexed
and the nation dispirited by Sir John Moore's retreat.
The Opposition also took the opportunity of de-
nouncing more violently than before the policy of
intervention on behalf of Spain and Portugal.   Napoleon, after making himself master of the whole of
Spain, had started in January for Paris, where he
began his preparations for another campaign against
Austria.   The British troops remaining in Portugal
under Sir John Craddock's command were left without funds or supplies, while they were threatened on
the north by Soult's occupation of Oporto and on the
east by the presence of Victor's army in the Tagus

valley. At one time the Cabinet had almost decided to withdraw from the Peninsula, but before issuing orders to that effect they consulted General Wellesley, who, in a convincing memorandum, urged on the Government the feasibility of defending Portugal, and of training the Portuguese troops under the super-intendence of British officers, so as to render them capable of facing the French. He pointed out that a defence of this nature would be extremely useful to the Spaniards in their contest with France, and that it could be effected by the employment of a British force of about 30,000 men, provided that England was prepared to afford very extensive pecuniary assistance and strong political support to the Portuguese nation and that the organisation and control of the Portu-guese army was placed entirely in the hands of the British commander. These views commended them-selves to His Majesty's Ministers, the more so as the certainty of an early rupture between France and Austria encouraged them to persevere in their struggle against Napoleon ; but still they were by no means con-fident of success, or disposed to devote all the energies and resources of the nation to the vigorous prosecution of the policy which Wellesley recommended.

In choosing an officer for the chief command in the Peninsula, a difference of opinion appears to have

arisen in the Cabinet; but eventually Wellesley's
high military reputation and great social and political
influence carried the day, and the Government entrusted him with the duty of giving effect to his own
proposals. He accordingly resigned the office of
Chief Secretary for Ireland in April 1809, and at once
proceeded to Lisbon, where he took over the command from Sir John Craddock. A month before,
Major-General Beresford, who had been appointed to
the command of the Portuguese forces with the local
rank of Marshal, had arrived, and begun his re-
organisation by selecting British officers for all the
more important military posts. With the help of
these officers and by his own tact and ability he
gradually raised the Portuguese troops to a high
standard of discipline and efficiency. General Wellesley had the chief command of the Portuguese as well
as of the British army, and in July 1809 he was given
the rank of Marshal-General in the Portuguese service.

Napoleon, on leaving Spain, had given orders to his
generals to continue the operations he had begun,
with the object of driving the English out of the
Peninsula, and bringing the whole country into sub-
jection. Soult was directed to occupy Oporto by
February 5th, on which date he was to instruct
General Lapisse, who commanded a division at

Salamanca, to march upon Ciudad Rodrigo and Abrantes. Reinforced by Lapisse, Marshal Victor, who was stationed in the Tagus valley, was to threaten Lisbon from the east, while Soult was to advance upon that city from the north. As soon as

SIR JOHN MOORE.

Lisbon had been captured, and the British force compelled to evacuate Portugal, Soult was to place a portion of his troops at Victor's disposal, and the latter, operating through Merida, was to make himself master of Seville. This plan was ably conceived,

but depended for its success on the promptitude with
which it was carried out by the French commanders,
and on their being able to overcome the resistance of
the British army. Soult's troops had been greatly
fatigued by their rapid pursuit of Sir John Moore,
and consequently were unable to occupy Oporto
before the end of March. Victor, however, on the
28th of that month defeated the Spanish general,
Cuesta, with immense slaughter, at Medellin, east of
Merida ; and the following day a French division,
under Sebastiani, routed another Spanish force at
Ciudad Real, about a hundred miles south of Madrid.
Lapisse, instead of moving towards Abrantes on the
Tagus, joined Victor on the Guadiana at Merida on
April 19th. The French, therefore, were exceedingly
strong in Spanish Estremadura ; but, owing to the
Emperor's instructions, Victor awaited Soult's advance
on Lisbon before crossing the Portuguese frontier.

When Wellesley landed on April 22nd he perceived
that Soult and Victor were too far apart to afford
each other mutual support, and that he had it in his
power to act against either. He considered it of
primary importance to expel the French from Oporto,
and thus carry out his scheme of maintaining the
integrity of Portugal, and using that country as a
base of operations against the French in Spain.

After taking the necessary steps to prevent, or at any rate to retard, any movement that Victor might attempt in the direction of Lisbon, Wellesley rapidly concentrated his force, consisting of 13,000 British, 3000 German, and 9000 Portuguese soldiers, at Coimbra, and, marching in two columns, reached the Douro on May 12th. He found Soult's army in occupation of Oporto, separated from him by a deep and rapid river, three hundred and twenty yards in width. He possessed no bridge equipment, and all the country boats had been removed to the right bank of the stream. Massing his artillery on a height which commanded a strongly walled enclosure on the opposite bank, he directed Captain Waters, a staff officer of unrivalled activity and resource, to procure some boats in which a crossing could be effected. Captain Waters was fortunate enough to discover an old boat hidden among the rushes and filled with mud. In this, aided by a few peasants, he managed to cross the river, and finding four barges with no guard over them on the enemy's side, he succeeded in bringing them away without attracting attention. Detaching a column under General John Murray to cross the river at Avintas, three miles above Oporto, and thus threaten the French line of retreat, the British commander managed to send over troops sufficient to hold the walled enclosure before the enemy realised his intention ; other boats were procured from up-stream ; the river was crossed at several points ; and eventually the French were driven out of Oporto with such rapidity and in such confusion that General Wellesley at four o'clock that afternoon dined at the table which had been prepared for Marshal Soult. General Murray failed to attack the French flank in conformity with his instructions. Had he done so, a large portion of the retreating force would have been destroyed. As it was, Oporto fell into the hands of the English, and Soult was compelled to retire through Braga on Orense in Galicia, where he arrived on May 19th with only 18,000 men, having lost 6000 killed, wounded, and prisoners, as well as his guns, ammunition, baggage, stores, and military chest.

Having thus for the time disposed of Soult, Wellesley turned his attention towards Victor's army quartered in the valley of the Upper Tagus ; and this was the more necessary as General Lapisse had seized the bridge over the Tagus at Alcantara, and Soult, after reorganising and re-equipping his troops, was beginning to move in a south-easterly direction to Zamora on the Upper Douro, with the object of reinforcing Madrid. In transferring his operations to

the south, Wellesley had serious difficulties to overcome. The rapid march from Lisbon to Oporto, and
thence in pursuit of Soult, had sent over 4000 of his
men into hospital; provisions were scarce; the
soldiers' shoes and clothing were in bad order ; their
discipline had been impaired by success ; and money
was not forthcoming, either to pay the troops or to
purchase supplies. Moreover, Cuesta, who was in
chief command of the Spanish army, refused to act as
Wellesley recommended. The result was that the
British force was detained in the neighbourhood of
Abrantes until the end of June. Wellesley had about
22,000 men at his disposal, while Cuesta's army, with
its headquarters at Oropesa, numbered about 33,000.
The French had 250,000 soldiers in the Peninsula, but
out of these only 50,000 were immediately available
to oppose the British advance, 33,000 being under
Victor, 12,000 under Sebastiani, and 5000 under
Joseph. At the end of June, Soult, then at Zamora,
received orders from Napoleon to take up a position
north of the Tagus valley, and, as soon as Wellesley
had committed himself to a forward movement, to
cross the mountains and fall on his flank and rear.
On July 20th the British troops joined Cuesta's army
at Oropesa, and it was arranged that the combined
force should advance towards Madrid, while Venegas,

with another Spanish column 26,000 strong, should
approach the capital from the south through Toledo
and Aranjuez.   Venegas failed to march at the
appointed time, and the French army was able to
concentrate undisturbed at and near Toledo from the
24th to the 26th July.   On the 22nd Wellesley
entered Talavera, and wished to attack Victor the
next day, before the troops under Sebastiani and
the king had come up.   But Cuesta refused on
the ground that July 23rd was a Sunday.   On the
24th Soult received orders from Joseph to move
at once from Salamanca on Plasencia, but he obeyed
in such a dilatory manner that the three corps
under his command were not assembled in the
Tagus valley until August 5th.   On July 27th Victor
attacked the British and Spanish forces, which
were drawn up on the right bank of the Tagus, with
their right flank resting on Talavera.   The Spaniards
in front of that flank were defeated, and fled with
their artillery many miles to the rear, only 4000 out
of a corps of 10,000 returning to the field of battle.
On the left flank the British troops held their own.
The next day Victor renewed the combat.   Sir
Arthur was watching the advance of the French,
when Colonel Donkin was sent by the Spanish
general Albuquerque to report that Cuesta had made

BATTLE OF TALAVERA.

To face p. 76.

terms with the enemy. With immovable coolness
Wellesley read the letter, desired Colonel Donkin to
return to his brigade, and continued his own reconnaissance. At two o'clock in the afternoon the battle
began, Victor's object being to turn the left and break
through the centre of the British line. In this he
failed, owing not only to his opponent's readiness of
resource and tactical skill, but also to the surpassing
gallantry of the British soldiers. In this engagement
the British loss exceeded 6000 killed and wounded,
inclusive of five general officers, and that of the
French was over 7000. "The battle of Talavera,"
says Jomini, "restored to the successors of Marlborough the glory which for a whole age seemed to
have passed from them," and it caused Napoleon to
change his opinion regarding the bravery of British
troops and the capacity of their leaders. The next
day the two armies remained in presence of each
other, but the British were reinforced by the celebrated Light Division, 3000 strong, under General
Crauford, which in twenty-six hours accomplished a
march of sixty-two miles, and, although each soldier
carried a load of from fifty to sixty pounds on his
back, left only seventeen stragglers behind. On
July 30th Joseph became anxious about the safety of
Madrid, and fell back on the Alberche, and shortly

afterwards Wellesley received information that Soult, with 37,000 men, had reached Plasencia with the intention of cutting him off from his base. It had been arranged with Cuesta that the mountain passes giving access to Plasencia should be guarded by Spanish troops, but these had fled on the ap-

MAJOR-GENERAL BERESFORD.

proach of the French columns without firing a shot. Wellesley now found himself in an extremely critical position, being threatened in front and rear by forces equal or superior to his own ; he could place no reliance on his Spanish Allies ; and his own army was almost starving, owing to the failure of the local authorities to provide the supplies and transport which they had promised. He extricated himself, however, by a rapid march, crossed the Tagus at Arzobispo, arrested Soult's advance by breaking down the bridge of boats at Almaraz, and retired through Truxillo and Merida on Badajoz and Elvas. The enemy attempted nothing further, and the several corps soon separated, their leaders being unable to agree upon a united course of action. This expedition taught Wellington that he had to face the same difficulties which baffled Sir John Moore. In Brialmont's words, it showed him "the ignorance and wrongheadedness of the Spanish generals ; the worthlessness of their troops ; the blind hostility of the Juntas ; the apathy of the Spanish people; their insane hatred of the Portuguese : and their unsatisfactory disposition towards the English soldiers, with whom they were never on good terms." Thenceforward up to the end of the war Wellesley wisely resolved to act independently, and to rely on his own resources and his own soldiers.

In August 1809 Sir Arthur Wellesley was created a peer with the titles of Baron Douro of Wellesley and Viscount Wellington of Talavera, and in the succeeding February he received the thanks of Parliament and a pension of £2000 a year for three lives. This pension was strongly opposed by the Corporation of London, the Common Council representing that Wellington "had exhibited in the campaign of Talavera, with equal rashness and ostentation, nothing but a useless valour." The grant was also censured by the Opposition in both Houses of Parliament.

Returning to Lisbon in October 1809, Wellington gave orders for the construction of the celebrated defensive works at Torres Vedras. He afterwards visited Seville and Cadiz, where he met his brother, the Marquis Wellesley, who had been appointed ambassador at the seat of the provisional Spanish Government. Towards the close of the year the main body of the British troops was transferred from Badajoz and Elvas to the Mondego valley, and General Hill was left at Abrantes to guard the valley of the Lower Tagus. In the meantime the French Emperor, having made peace with Austria, ordered 100,000 men to be collected on the Spanish frontier, and proposed, early in 1810, to lead them himself into Spain. In November 1809 the Spanish armies were signally defeated at Ocaña by Marshal Mortier, and at Alba de Tormes by General Kellermann ; and in January 1810 Joseph invaded Andalusia, overran the whole province, and captured Seville. Napoleon was so much occupied with public and private affairs, especially with his negotiations for a marriage with a Russian or Austrian Princess, that he abandoned the idea of personally directing the operations in the Peninsula ; but he sent large reinforcements into the country, and appointed Soult to the chief command in Spain, while Marshal Masséna was selected to lead an army into Portugal.

In England the nation had been mortified by the failure of the Walcheren expedition, and the hospitals were crowded with soldiers suffering from the Walcheren fever. Recruits could hardly be obtained even by the offer of high bounties, and the expenses of the war were causing grave financial embarrassment. A disagreement between Mr. Canning and Lord Castlereagh was followed by a duel and by the dissolution of the Portland Ministry. Another Government was formed under Mr. Perceval, in which Lord Liverpool replaced Lord Castlereagh as Secretary for War. Wellington perceived that the new Cabinet was disposed to withdraw the British army from the Peninsula, and, as he did not wish to give any pretext for such a decision, he refrained from asking for the reinforcements and supplies which might have enabled him to defend the Portuguese frontier. His plan was gradually to fall back on the Torres Vedras lines, and to take measures for laying waste the districts in which the French army would operate. Stringent orders were given that the people should be compelled to destroy their mills and bridges, drive away their cattle, abandon their homes, and carry with them everything that could be made use of by an invading force. As a result of these measures, the French troops, who lived by requisition and plunder, would starve in front of Lisbon, and would be obliged to retreat or disperse in order to obtain food and forage.

In June 1810, Masséna, with 80,000 men under his orders, began the campaign by besieging Ciudad Rodrigo; and although the Portuguese and Spanish authorities entreated Wellington to march to its relief, he steadfastly refused to do so. Ciudad Rodrigo surrendered early in July, and Almeida was next invested. This fortress was expected to make an obstinate defence, but owing to the explosion of the main magazine it became untenable, and had to be given up after a short siege. The possession of these places furnished the French commander with good bases for offensive action, and at the beginning of September he marched towards Viseu, which he reached on the 21st. Wellington had meanwhile concentrated his force in the Mondego valley, and resolved to dispute the passage of that river. His reasons for engaging the enemy were, first, that his army was dispirited by the fall of Ciudad Rodrigo and Almeida, and required a victory to restore its confidence; and, secondly, that the devastation of the country in front of Lisbon was not yet completed.

LORD CASTLEREAGH.

He accordingly took up a position on the Sierra de Busaco, where the enemy, about 56,000 strong, attacked him on September 27th, but were repulsed with much slaughter. The French loss in this engagement amounted to 4500 killed and wounded; that of

G 2

the British and Portuguese to about 1300. After the battle Masséna drew off towards the sea, and continued his advance through Coimbra upon Leiria by the coast road, while Wellington retired by easy marches through Condeixa and Leiria to Torres Vedras. The French had hardly quitted the Mondego when their line of communication with Almeida was interrupted by a detachment of Portuguese Militia, and shortly afterwards a similar force surprised the garrison of Coimbra and captured Masséna's depôts and a large number of his wounded. On October 10th, the French Marshal found himself in front of the triple line of entrenchments, which had been constructed with such secrecy that, until he reached them, he was absolutely unaware of their existence. The lines, defended by about 30,000 men and 250 guns, were impregnable, and the country around them was a desert. Masséna might at once have retreated, or he might have crossed the Tagus, threatened Lisbon from the left bank of that river, and based his further operations on Spanish Estremadura, where supplies were plentiful. He did neither, and his army soon became demoralised by inactivity and starvation. Towards the end of October he found it necessary to establish his headquarters at Santarem, while Wellington remained within the

Torres Vedras entrenchments, which he strengthened from day to day, and completed by a line of works on the left bank of the Tagus. Masséna sent General Foy to make an urgent appeal to Napoleon for assistance, but the Emperor was preparing for the invasion of Russia, and refused to supply the reinforcements asked for. He gave orders, however, to Marshal Soult, who was then occupied in besieging Cadiz, to march a force about 30,000 strong towards Abrantes, and desired his brother Joseph to push forward in the direction of Alcantara. Soult was disinclined to move; nevertheless, he slowly collected a siege train and, advancing northward, captured Merida, Olivença, and Badajoz, which were held by Spanish garrisons. Shortly after the surrender of Badajoz, which took place on March 11th, 1811, Soult heard that the English were attempting the relief of Cadiz, and he therefore returned to Andalusia. Towards the end of February Masséna found it impossible to maintain his position at Santarem, and on March 2nd the French army began its retreat, destroying, as it marched, the baggage, ammunition, horses and guns which impeded its progress, burning the towns through which it passed, and putting many of the inhabitants to death. Wellington, who during the winter had received reinforcements from England, followed the enemy on March 7th, and attacked the French rear-guard commanded by Ney at Pombal on the 11th, at Redinha on the 12th, at Cazal Nova on the 14th, and at the passage of the Ceira on the 15th. On arriving at Celorico and Guarda, Masséna, whose troops now only numbered 40,000, proposed to march southwards to the Tagus valley at Alcantara, and there to recommence operations against Lisbon, in conjunction with Soult and Joseph. Ney refused to comply, and after a sharp altercation between the two marshals, Masséna removed him from his command, and appointed General Loison to take his place. But before the French army could evade the pursuit of the British force, Wellington crossed the Guarda mountains, and forced the enemy to retire across the Coa on Sabugal, where, on April 3rd, he attacked and defeated Reynier's corps, which was holding that town. The next day the French crossed the Portuguese frontier, and four days afterwards Masséna passed through Ciudad Rodrigo, where he left a division, and fell back on Salamanca. During this campaign the Marshal had lost 30,000 men, and had been defeated in every action in which his troops had been engaged. The miseries which Portugal endured on this occasion, rather than submit to the rule of Napoleon, are thus described by Colonel Jones, R.E.,

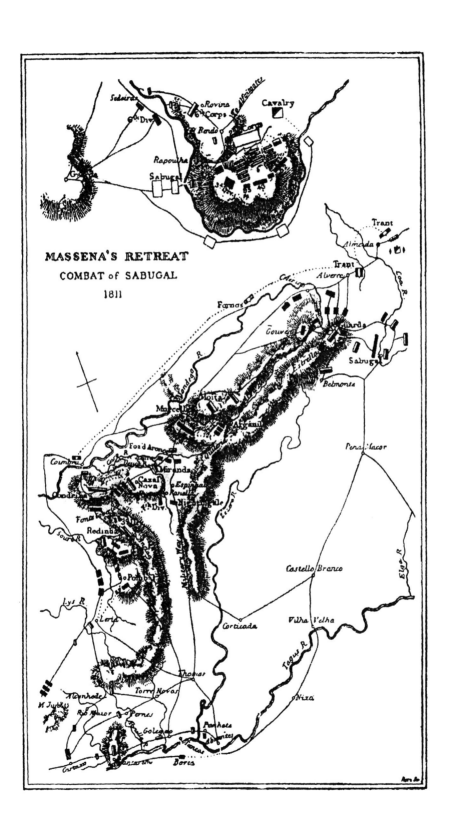

MASSENA'S RETREAT

COMBAT of SABUGAL

1811

who was serving with the British force :—"Nearly two thousand square miles of country remained for five months with scarcely an inhabitant; everything it contained was devoured by the enemy, or destroyed by the season. In the space immediately bounding the positions of the two armies, not permanently occupied by either, the produce of the harvest perished, scattered over the ground, and the vintage mouldered on the stalk; flocks of innumerable small birds, drawn to the spot by instinct, fattened unmolested on the ungathered grapes; and latterly, the very wolves, conscious of security, or rendered more daring by the absence of their accustomed prey, prowled about, masters of the country, reluctantly giving way to the cavalry patrols which occasionally crossed their track."

The Perceval Ministry was much encouraged by the disastrous retreat of the French, and congratulated Wellington on the success of his defensive operations. He also received the thanks of Parliament for the liberation of Portugal.

During his pursuit of Masséna, Wellington heard of the surrender of Badajoz, and determined to detach Beresford for the purpose of investing that fortress and retaking Olivença. Beresford accordingly started on March 16th, with 20,000 infantry, 2000 cavalry,

and 18 guns, and reached Campo Mayor on the 25th;
but great delay occurred in crossing the Guadiana, as
the Spaniards had neglected to provide a bridge of
boats, and the only timber procurable was ill adapted
for the construction of a trestle bridge. Eventually
the troops had to cross the river upon rafts, an
operation which occupied three days, and gave the
French time to repair the defences of Badajoz, provision the place, and mount their artillery. As
Beresford approached, Marshal Mortier retreated
towards Seville, leaving a garrison in the fortress and
a detachment at Olivença. On April 21st, Wellington
arrived from the north, reconnoitred Badajoz, and
arranged with Beresford for its speedy capture. In
the meantime, however, Masséna had reorganised his
army at Salamanca, and, with the aid of such reinforcements as he could collect, attempted to relieve
Almeida, which had been invested by the British
army. Hearing of this movement, Wellington left
Badajoz, rejoined the main body of his troops, and
took up a position at Fuentes d'Onoro, between
Almeida and Ciudad Rodrigo. There on May 3rd
and 5th he successfully resisted the French onslaught,
the British and Portuguese losing about 1800 killed,
wounded, and prisoners, and the French 2700. On
May 6th, Masséna again fell back on Salamanca, and

in the night of the 10th, General Brennier, commanding the Almeida garrison, broke through the
investing force and rejoined the French army.
Shortly afterwards Napoleon removed Masséna from
his command, and replaced him by Marshal Marmont.

While these events were taking place in the north,
Beresford had begun the siege of Badajoz, and
hearing that Soult was marching to its relief with
19,000 infantry, 4000 cavalry, and 40 guns, he
determined to take up a position in advance of the
place. He accordingly moved to Albuera, where, on
the night of the 15th, he effected a junction with a
Spanish column under General Blake. The Spaniards
were worn out by fatigue and starvation, and their
leader was too conceited and obstinate to obey the
orders which were given him. The total force at
Beresford's disposal amounted to about 32,000, of
which number 7000 were British and 10,000 Portuguese. On the morning of May 16th Soult attacked
the Allies, and so nearly defeated them that Beresford was preparing to retreat. Luckily, however,
Colonel Hardinge, Quartermaster-General of the
Portuguese army, took upon himself to order the
advance of the Fusilier Brigade under General Cole,
and this movement turned the fortune of the day.
In the following passage, perhaps the most impressive

in his history, Napier records the surpassing gallantry of the British troops during the concluding phase of this combat. "Nothing could stop that astonishing infantry. No sudden burst of undisciplined valour, no nervous enthusiasm weakened the stability of their order; their flashing eyes were bent on the dark columns in their front, their measured tread shook the ground, their dreadful volleys swept away the head of every formation, their deafening shouts over-powered the dissonant cries that broke from all parts of the tumultuous crowd, as slowly and with a horrid carnage it was pushed by the incessant vigour of the attack to the farthest edge of the hill. In vain did the French reserves mix with the struggling multi-tude to sustain the fight,—their efforts only increased the irremediable confusion, and the mighty mass, breaking off like a loosened cliff, went headlong down the steep; the rain flowed after in streams discoloured with blood, and eighteen hundred unwounded men, the remnant of six thousand unconquerable British soldiers, stood triumphant on the fatal hill."

Soult's loss had been so heavy that the next day he remained inactive, and the day following he with-drew to await the arrival of reinforcements. Wel-lington, with two divisions, reached Elvas from the north on May 19th, and continued the siege of

Badajoz, Soult meanwhile establishing himself at Llerena, where, in the middle of June, he was joined by a column under Drouet, and subsequently by Marmont's force from Salamanca. His troops being greatly outnumbered, and an attempt to capture Badajoz by assault having failed, Wellington decided to raise the siege and to retire beyond the Caya. This operation was skilfully effected by June 19th, and shortly afterwards the French marshals separated, Soult going south to guard Seville against the attack of a Spanish force under Blake, and Marmont taking up a position on the Tagus between Talavera and Alcantara.

In July Wellington transferred the greater part of his army to the province of Beira, north of the Lower Tagus, with a view to surprising Ciudad Rodrigo ; but early in August the French provisioned that fortress for two months, and on September 23rd Marmont, who had moved to Salamanca, opened communications with the garrison and threw in eight months' supplies. Wellington, therefore, drew back from Ciudad Rodrigo to the position of El Bodon, where Marmont attacked him with his cavalry and artillery on September 25th. During this action a square formed of the 5th and 77th Foot was charged on three of its faces at the same moment without being broken. Although the English gained the day at El Bodon, Wellington's flank divisions had not come up, and he thought it expedient to retire towards the Coa. His outposts were attacked by Marmont at Aldea da Ponte without any decisive result, and the following day the French commander retreated, a portion of his troops returning to Salamanca and the rest to the Tagus valley. Thereupon the British force established itself on the Coa, with headquarters at Freneda, and renewed the blockade of Ciudad Rodrigo.

During the remainder of the year 1811 nothing further was attempted, but Napoleon withdrew a large proportion of his veterans from Spain for the invasion of Russia, replacing them by an equal number of young soldiers ; and Wellington secretly collected a bridge and siege train and other equipment necessary for the capture of Ciudad Rodrigo. Marmont, believing that the British force would remain inactive during the winter, had reduced the garrison of that place to 1800 men, when Wellington suddenly crossed the Agueda on January 7th, 1812, and began his investment the same day. The siege was vigorously conducted, and on the evening of the 19th the fortress was assaulted and captured by two columns led by Picton and Crauford. During

the siege and assault the Allies lost 90 officers and
1200 men killed and wounded, among the killed
being General Crauford. Three hundred of the
garrison were killed, and 80 officers and 1500 soldiers
taken prisoners. In the fortress were found an
immense quantity of ammunition and 150 guns,
including Marmont's siege train. In recognition of
his services on this occasion Wellington received an
earldom and an additional pension of £2000 a year;
he was also created a grandee of Spain with the title
of Duque de Ciudad Rodrigo.

While Marmont, under Napoleon's orders, was
collecting his troops at Salamanca, and preparing for
an advance on Almeida, Wellington resolved to lay
siege to Badajoz, and, transferring the greater part
of his army from Beira to the valley of the Guadiana,
invested that fortress on March 16th. Marmont was
anxious to co-operate with Soult in the defence of
Badajoz, but was warned by the French Emperor not
to interfere. The siege was pushed on in spite of
the tempestuous weather, swampy ground, interrupted
communications, and imperfect appliances. Soult,
believing that Badajoz was in no immediate danger,
began to assemble a large force at Llerena, but on
April 5th the breaches appeared to be practicable,
and Wellington decided to assault the place the

following evening. The issue was for some time doubtful, as the garrison, under General Philippon, defended themselves with great gallantry; but finally the heroic valour of the British troops overcame all resistance, and Badajoz was taken, with a loss to the besiegers of more than 5000 men, of whom over 3500 fell in the assault. Of the garrison only 1300 were killed or wounded. As soon as he had got possession of Badajoz, it had been Wellington's intention to operate against Soult's army at Llerena; but the neglect of the Spaniards to throw supplies into Ciudad Rodrigo, which was threatened by Marmont, obliged him to return to the north. Soult shortly afterwards fell back on Seville; and General Hill, having surprised the French and broken the bridge over the Tagus at Almaraz, severed the direct line of communication between that city and Madrid. Wellington then caused the bridge at Alcantara to be repaired, and took steps to improve the navigation of the Tagus and Douro, thus providing a short and secure line of communication between his troops on the Agueda and those in the Tagus valley, and connecting the Portuguese frontier with his bases on the seaboard.

When Marmont, who had advanced as far as Sabugal and Castello Branco, heard of the fate of

Badajoz and the subsequent movement of the British
troops in support of Ciudad Rodrigo, he withdrew to
Salamanca; and there Wellington determined to
attack him. Crossing the Agueda on June 13th, he
invested with one division the fortified posts which
Marmont had constructed in front of the city, while
with the remainder of his troops he operated against
the French army, which fell back on the Douro. The
strength of the defences having been underrated,
considerable delay occurred in reducing them, and
the French garrison did not surrender until June 27th,
ten days after the investment. During this interval
Marmont was reinforced, and took up a strong
position on the right bank of the Douro. Wellington
followed to the left bank, but found the enemy in
such strength, and was himself so embarrassed by the
want of money, and consequently of supplies, that he
contemplated a retreat to the Portuguese frontier.
Marmont resolved to assume the offensive; and,
suddenly crossing the Douro at Tordesillas on
July 17th, manœuvred for several days in close
proximity to the British army, his object being to
regain Salamanca and cut off his opponent's retreat.
The result of these manœuvres was generally favourable to the French, until on July 22nd Wellington,
seeing his opportunity while the enemy were engaged

in a complicated evolution, attacked and completely defeated them. Marmont had his arm broken and was severely wounded in the side, and Wellington was hit by a spent shot; the French lost about 6000

GENERAL LORD HILL, G.C.B.
After a painting by O. Dawe, R.A.

killed and wounded, including seven general officers, and the Allies over 5000, including six general officers. In recognition of this victory the Cortes conferred the order of the Golden Fleece on the British commander, and appointed him generalissimo

H

of the Spanish armies.   Wellington also received the
thanks of Parliament and a money grant of £100,000,
and was advanced in the peerage to the rank of
marquis.

General Clausel, who succeeded Marshal Marmont
in the command of the French army, fell back on
Burgos, and Wellington moved towards Madrid, which
he entered on August 12th, Joseph having retired
towards Valencia, where he ordered Soult to join him
with the army of Andalusia.   On September 1st
Wellington quitted Madrid, and, marching north,
drove Clausel out of Valladolid on the 7th, and on
the 18th occupied the town of Burgos.   The next day
he began the siege of the fortress of Burgos, which
was strong, heavily armed, and garrisoned by 1700
French soldiers under General Dubreton.   The place
held out for more than a month, and meanwhile
General Souham, who had been sent from France to
succeed Clausel, had collected a force of 40,000 strong
at Briviesca, while Soult, having joined Joseph at
Almanza, was advancing on Madrid.   On October
22nd Wellington raised the siege of Burgos, and on
the 29th he crossed the Douro and retreated upon
Salamanca.   At the same time General Hill fell back
from Madrid, and rejoined his chief on November 8th.
The French armies, under Soult and Souham, had

also united, and threatened to cut off their opponents
from Ciudad Rodrigo ; but Wellington, by a bold
flank march, evaded the enemy and reached the
Agueda on November 19th. There he halted for
some months, distributing his troops so as to guard
the Portuguese frontier ; the French withdrew at the
same time, and took up a position stretching from
Valladolid to Toledo.

During the winter the British Government sent out
considerable reinforcements to the Peninsula, and
Wellington, having reorganised the Portuguese army,
did his best to improve the administration of the
Spanish army, and to prepare for an advance in the
spring. On the other hand, the condition of the
French troops rapidly deteriorated. Napoleon continued to withdraw more of his old soldiers, replacing
them by untrained conscripts ; and such differences
of opinion arose between the King and his military
advisers that no comprehensive scheme of action
could be decided on. Joseph was so much offended
by Soult's opposition to his views that, in writing to
the Emperor, he declared, "Either the Duke of
Dalmatia must quit Spain or I will." The ablest
French commander in the Peninsula was accordingly
recalled, and placed at the head of the Imperial
Guard in Germany. Napoleon sent orders to Joseph

to move his court from Madrid to Valladolid, and
there to concentrate the armies of the south, the
centre, and Portugal, so as to be ready to fight if the
Allied force attempted to advance upon France.
These instructions reached Joseph by the middle of
February 1813, but his movements were so dilatory
that he was not established at Valladolid until the
beginning of April, and even then his armies, instead
of being concentrated, were dispersed over a wide
extent of country. The King imagined that Wellington's first object would be to occupy Madrid, and the
British commander encouraged this belief by false
reports and deceptive movements. He had fully resolved, however, to operate through the northern
provinces, where he had ready access to the sea,
where the Spanish troops from Galicia and the
Asturias were capable of rendering very material
assistance, and where the defeat of the French army
would sever its communication with France, and thus
necessitate its withdrawal to the Pyrenees.

On May 15th the left wing of the British army, numbering about 40,000 men, under Sir Thomas Graham,
crossed the Lower Douro, and marched through the
Tras-os-Montes towards the Esla. On the 22nd, the
right wing, 38,000 strong, began its advance through
Salamanca on Zamora. On the 31st the left wing

forded the Esla, and the next day Zamora was occupied, and the junction between the two wings secured. Wellington's force now amounted to 70,000 British and Portuguese, and 8000 Spanish soldiers from Estremadura. The number of the latter was raised to 20,000 on June 3rd by a reinforcement of 12,000 Galicians from Benavente. To this force the King could only oppose 35,000 infantry, and 10,000 cavalry, and he was therefore obliged to retire from Valladolid to Burgos. Wellington followed the French closely, and by threatening their right, induced Joseph to evacuate Burgos, a fortress which a few months before had successfully resisted the whole British army. Crossing the Ebro, the King took up a strong position where he might await reinforcements and dispute the enemy's passage ; but Wellington moved rapidly to his own left by roads believed to be impracticable, crossed the river unopposed by bridges higher up the stream, and established a new base at Santander. On the evening of June 18th, the French staff received the news that their right flank had been turned, and in confusion and dismay the army was withdrawn the same night by a forced march to Vittoria. Arrived at Vittoria, Joseph did nothing for several days, except to send away a convoy of stores and sick under an escort of 4000 men. On the 21st Wellington attacked and routed the enemy at Vittoria, capturing 150 out of 152 guns, all the French ammunition, their public and private baggage, and one million sterling of treasure; also the pictures, jewellery, and other plunder which the King and his generals were carrying out of Spain. Marshal Jourdan's baton was found in the King's carriage, and was presented by Wellington to the Prince Regent, who gave him in exchange the baton of a British Field Marshal. The French loss on this day amounted to 6000, and that of the Allies to about 5200. Joseph retreated through Pamplona, the garrison of which he strengthened, and General Foy retiring through Tolosa threw a detachment of good troops into San Sebastian. With the exception of these garrisons and of the force in Valencia and Catalonia, commanded by Marshal Suchet, the French army had been driven out of Spain.

When Napoleon, who was at Dresden, heard of Wellington's success, he ordered Soult to start at once for Paris, and having there conferred with the War Minister, to continue his journey to the Spanish frontier. On his arrival he was to assume the chief command, and, as arrangements were being made to supply him with a reinforcement of nearly 100,000 men, the Emperor hoped that he would be able to make head against the British, Portuguese and Spanish forces. Soult left Dresden on July 1st, reached Bayonne on the 12th, and on the 25th marched on Pamplona. Sir Thomas Graham had begun the siege of San Sebastian on the 10th, but was repulsed in his attempt to take the fortress by assault on the 25th. Wellington thereupon converted the siege into a blockade, and turned his attention to the right of his line, which was threatened by the French Marshal. Concentrating the right and centre divisions near Pamplona, he stopped the enemy's advance by a series of very skilful manœuvres. On July 28th he defeated Soult at Sorauren ; and on August 2nd the Allied troops reoccupied the position on the Pyrenees, from which they had temporarily fallen back. San Sebastian was taken by a second assault on August 31st, and the garrison capitulated on September 8th, after a most gallant defence of the castle or retrenchment to which it had retired. The loss to the Allies in killed and wounded during the second assault exceeded 2500 men, among the killed being Colonel Fletcher, the Chief Engineer ; and the total loss throughout the siege and blockade was not less than 5600. The garrison commanded by General Rey numbered 3000, of whom over 1700 were killed or wounded.

On October 7th Wellington took Soult by surprise,

and crossed the Bidassoa with the same skill as he
had displayed in crossing the Douro in May 1809.
By this movement the British force turned the right
of the French and forced them back on the Nivelle.
On October 31st Pamplona surrendered, and on
November 10th the whole Allied army invaded
France, driving the enemy out of their fortified positions on the Nivelle, and capturing 51 guns, much
ammunition, and many prisoners.   On December 9th
Wellington crossed the Nive, and during the four
succeeding days fought and repulsed Soult, who
attacked first the left and then the right of the British
army.   During this prolonged conflict, the Allies lost
about 4600 men, killed and wounded, and the French
5800, besides three German regiments which deserted
to the British side on the evening of the 10th.   Leaving
two divisions under Sir John Hope to blockade
Bayonne, the British commander followed up Soult's
retreat, and on February 27th, 1814, attacked and
defeated him on the Gave de Pau at Orthez.   From
the 24th to the 26th of the same month, the naval
squadron, under Admiral Penrose, assisted in throwing
a bridge over the Adour below Bayonne—a wonderful
feat, considering that the river was deep, rapid, subject
to the action of strong tides, defended by a flotilla of
gunboats and a large body of troops on the right

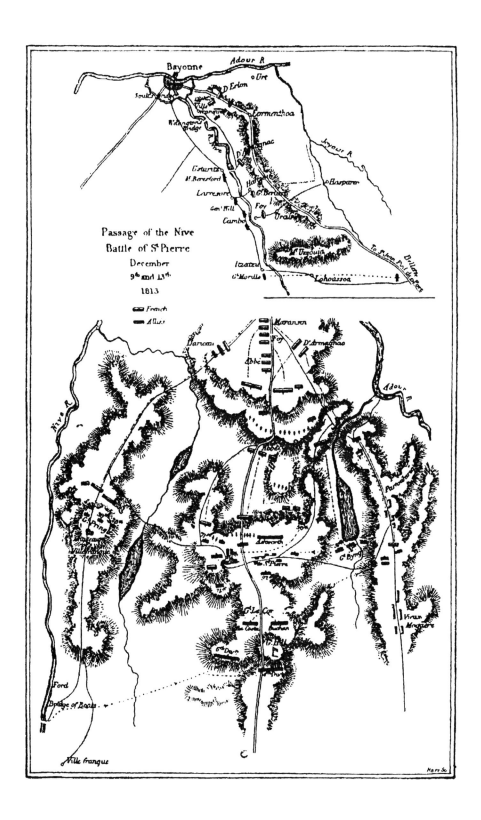

Passage of the Nive
Battle of St Pierre
December
9th and 13th
1813

French
Allies

bank, and 360 yards wide at the point of crossing. The bridge being completed, Bayonne was closely invested, and Soult drew off in the direction of Toulouse. Wellington crossed the Adour at St. Sever on March 1st, and on the 8th he detached two divisions under Beresford to occupy Bordeaux. Soult attempted to resume the offensive on March 13th, but was repulsed with such vigour that he fell back through Tarbes on Toulouse, where the last battle of the Peninsular War was fought on April 10th. In this final engagement the French lost 3200 killed and wounded, and the Allies 4600, of whom about 2000 were Spaniards. On each side four generals were wounded. The next day Soult withdrew from Toulouse, leaving eight guns and his wounded behind, and the day following the town was occupied by the British force. Napoleon having abdicated, and the Bourbon dynasty being replaced on the throne of France, the war came to an end.

On April 21st Wellington issued a general order thanking his troops for "their uniform discipline and gallantry in the field, and for their conciliating conduct towards the inhabitants of the country." Shortly afterwards the British army was broken up, the cavalry marching through France and embarking at Boulogne, and the infantry embarking at Bordeaux.

Only a portion of the latter returned to the United Kingdom, many gallant soldiers being sent to perish at New Orleans or to die of yellow fever in the West Indies.

On May 3rd, 1814, Wellington, who a year before had been made a Knight of the Garter, was advanced in the peerage to the dignity of a duke, and in the following month he was granted by Parliament a further sum of £400,000.

During the second phase of Wellington's career the qualities which he most conspicuously displayed were soundness of judgment, tenacity of purpose, and self-control. He had made up his mind that the best way of beating the French was not to be afraid of them. Just before he left England for Portugal, in 1808, he remarked : " The French have beaten all the world, and are supposed to be invincible. They have besides, it seems, a new system, which has out-manœuvred and overwhelmed all the armies of Europe. But no matter, my die is cast. They may overwhelm, but I don't think they will outmanœuvre me. In the first place, I am not afraid of them, as everybody else seems to be ; and secondly, if what I hear of their system of manœuvres be true, I think it a false one against troops steady enough, as I hope mine are, to receive them with the bayonet. I suspect that all the Continental armies were more than half beaten before the battle began."

In the second place, he was determined not to run any great risk of disaster, generally to adopt a defensive attitude, and only to fight when he felt reasonably certain of success. He fully appreciated the difference between the French system of conscription and the English system of voluntary enlistment; and he knew that under the latter the home Government could not be expected to make good the heavy losses which the French Emperor was in a position to disregard. On this point he observed, with reference to a plan of operations which had been submitted for his consideration : " The scheme might answer well enough if I could afford, or the British Government or nation would allow, of my being as prodigal of men as every French general is. They forget, however, that we have but one army, and that the same men who fought at Vimeiro and Talavera fought the other day at Sorauren ; and that, if I am to preserve that army, I must proceed with caution. Indeed, this becomes doubly necessary, as I see that, notwithstanding the fondness of the British nation for the sport, they began to cry out the other day upon the loss of 300 or 400 men in the unsuccessful storm of San Sebastian."

Then, again, he perceived how advisable it was to avoid the Continental system of making war support war. And this for two reasons. First, because troops fed by forced requisitions or plunder in such a country as Spain or Portugal would inevitably suffer such privations as gravely to impair their efficiency and diminish their numbers; and, secondly, because it was essential to secure the confidence and good-will of the civil population. In all his operations Wellington paid unremitting attention to his commissariat arrangements, kept his troops within easy distance of his bases on the seaboard, and carefully protected his lines of communication. From 1809 until the spring of 1813 he made use of Lisbon and Oporto as his principal centres of supply and reinforcement; and when he began his advance upon the Pyrenees, he established his depôts, magazines, and hospitals at Santander and other ports on the northern coast of Spain. His lines of communication being shorter and safer than those of the French, and funds or credit being available for the purchase of such stores as could not be imported from England, the British soldiers were better fed, clothed, and equipped than their opponents. In a letter dated January 26th, 1811, to his brother, the Marquis Wellesley, Wellington estimated the yearly casualties among the French

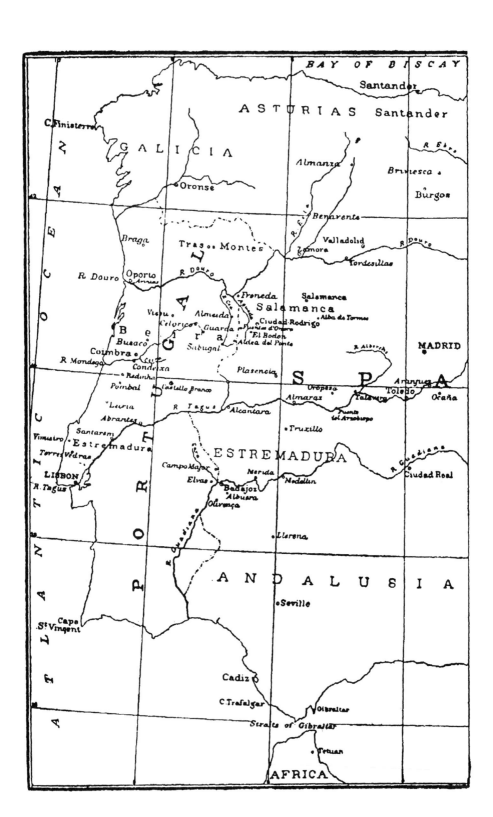

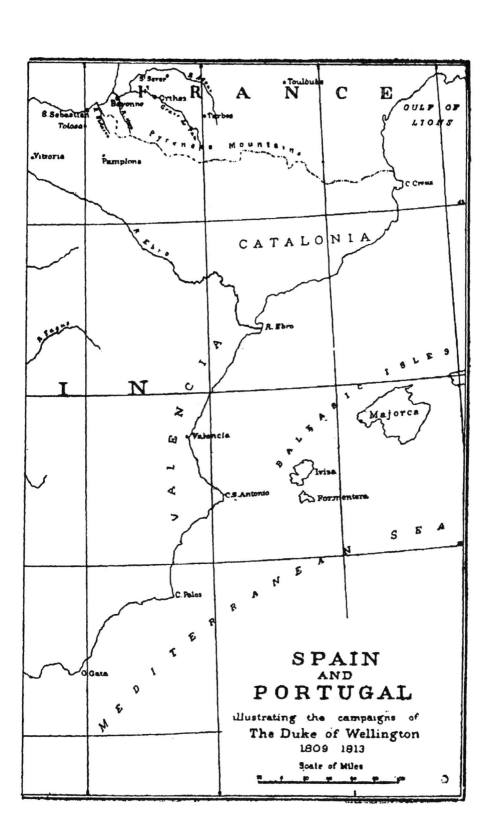

SPAIN
AND
PORTUGAL

Illustrating the campaigns of
The Duke of Wellington
1809 1813

Scale of Miles

troops on field service, due to the want of a properly organised commissariat, at not less than one-half. He said : " The French army is certainly a wonderful machine ; but if we are to form such a one, we must form such a government as exists in France, which can with impunity lose one-half of the troops employed in the field every year only by the privations and hardships imposed upon them."

Another conspicuous instance of Wellington's sound judgment was the conclusion he arrived at that Portugal was a country capable of being defended by a moderate number of troops, and likely to furnish the most advantageous base for operating against the French in Spain. Portugal being long and narrow, and provided with good harbours and two navigable waterways, the British communications were short and direct ; depôts could be formed unknown to the enemy on either the Tagus or the Douro ; and the French, having no means of ascertaining the probable direction of attack, were generally surprised and defeated before they could concentrate all their available forces. Moreover, the Portuguese were too much opposed to the French and the Spaniards to be unfriendly to the English. They allowed their soldiers to be trained and commanded by British officers, their foreign and internal policy was guided by the British Minister, and they even consented to abandon their homes and lay waste their fields in order to deprive their invaders of the means of subsistence.

Wellington's tenacity of purpose was evinced by his steady adherence to the policy which he regarded as likely to prove successful. He was determined to run no unnecessary risk, to spare his troops as much as possible, and never to compromise his communications by a too bold or too hasty advance. When feebly supported by the British Government, when funds and reinforcements were denied him, and when he was menaced by the enemy in apparently over-whelming strength, he never wavered in his resolve to hold on to Portugal, and thence to resume the offensive as soon as a fitting opportunity offered. He was equally firm and prudent when he had gained some great victory, and the British public clamoured for the immediate expulsion of the French from the Peninsula. On one occasion—after the battle of Tala-vera—he was very nearly cut off from his base, owing to a mistaken reliance on the co-operation of the Spanish troops. Thus taught a lesson which Sir John Moore had to learn at the expense of his life, he thenceforward trusted entirely to himself, although he continued to treat the Spanish generals with courtesy

and forbearance, and to make what use he could of
the soldiers under their command.

Nothing is more remarkable than Wellington's self-
control in dealing with his own subordinates, and with
the provisional governments of Portugal and Spain.
During the most critical period of the war, several of
his generals, who regarded it as hopeless to continue
the struggle, not only freely expressed their opinion
on the subject, but went home on leave, and used all
their parliamentary influence to procure the withdrawal of the British army. The two most influential
members of the Portuguese Government, Principal
Souza and the Bishop of Oporto, formed a party
hostile to the British, neglected to pay or feed the
Portuguese troops, wrote anonymous threatening
letters to Wellington, and made arrangements for
libelling and caricaturing him in England. In a letter
to Sir Charles Stuart, dated July 20th, 1813, he
remarked : "I must say that the British army, which
I have 'the honour to command, have met with
nothing but ingratitude from the Government and
authorities in Portugal for their services." The
Spanish Government was actuated by an equally
hostile spirit. On July 2nd, 1813, Wellington addressed Don Juan O'Donoju, the Spanish Secretary
for War, in the following terms :—"You are aware of

my disposition and desire still to serve the Spanish nation as far as is in my power. There are limits, however, to forbearance and submission to injury; and I confess that I feel that I have been most unworthily treated in these transactions by the Spanish Government, even as a gentleman." Writing four months later to his brother Henry about the attack made upon him by the Spanish Press, with reference to the siege of San Sebastian, he observed :—" The only reason why I noticed the libel in the *Duende* was, that it affected Sir Thomas Graham and the officers of the army ; and I was convinced that it was written under the direction of that greatest of all blackguards, the Minister at War." Wellington was naturally a man of strong temper, and no doubt felt extreme annoyance at the intrigues which endangered his plans, and the obstacles placed in his way by those to whom he had a right to look for assistance and support. But he was too great a man to show his feelings ; he recognised that every prominent servant of the state must be exposed to envy and detraction ; and he treated scheming generals and factious politicians with equal forbearance, and probably with equal contempt.

It is impossible, within the limits of a magazine article, to discuss the merits of Wellington's strategy and tactics during the Peninsular War. Suffice it to say that, generally with inferior numbers, and always with a mixed, and therefore a not altogether reliable force, composed partly of British and partly of Portuguese and Spanish troops, he met and defeated the ablest of Napoleon's marshals. He appears to have developed in the course of a five years' campaign tactical ability of the highest order; and, commanding as he did a body of veteran soldiers inured to war, and well trained in musketry and fire discipline, he displayed supreme military genius in being the first to recognise the advantages of an extended order of attack. Writing in April 1811 to Captain Chapman, R.E., he remarked:—"We have given the French a handsome dressing, and I think they will not say again that we are not a manœuvring army. We may not manœuvre so beautifully as they do; but I do not desire better sport than to meet one of their columns *en masse* with our lines."

As a strategist he knew his own mind and kept his own counsel. The passage of the Douro and occupation of Oporto, the retirement into the lines of Torres Vedras, the capture of Ciudad Rodrigo and Badajoz, and the advance through the Tras-os-Montes before the battle of Vittoria, are instances of masterly combinations which took the enemy entirely by

surprise. Wellington's sieges have often been criti-
cised on account of their occasional failure and the
great loss of life which attended them even when
successful. The fact is, however, that the appliances
and ordnance for siege operations were very defective ;
few, if any, sappers were attached to the British army,
and the enemy being generally more numerous than
the besieging force, and only wanting time to concentrate, the places could not be taken at all unless they
were taken quickly. Wellington, therefore, had no
choice in the matter. He was obliged to sacrifice his
soldiers in order to avoid the delay which would have
defeated his plans, and to compensate for deficiencies
in skilled labour and siege equipment. Another
point, on which considerable stress is laid by General
Brialmont and other writers, is the alleged failure of
Wellington to follow up his victories by vigorous
pursuits. Here again he appears to be blamed somewhat unreasonably. His army was a small one, the
British Government supplied him with reinforcements
in a sparing and dilatory manner, and, whenever
discipline was relaxed by success, the British soldiers
were liable to get out of hand and to disperse in
search of plunder. This tendency was strikingly
exemplified after the battle of Vittoria, when for
eighteen days 12,500 men were absent from the

colours, engaged in marauding among the mountains.

The success which attended Wellington's operations in the Peninsula is to be ascribed not only to his own military and administrative genius, and to the coolness, courage, and obstinacy of his troops, but also to the fact that the control of the British and Portuguese forces was centred in one man, who also exercised a predominant influence over the provisional governments of Spain and Portugal. However able a number of officers may be—and there can be no question as to the ability of the French marshals—they cannot be expected to think alike, or, if given co-ordinate authority, to act in unison. Napoleon's disinclination to appoint a supreme head over the French armies in Spain caused jealousy, vacillation, and confusion. The Emperor himself sent orders which, being written at a distance and in ignorance of the course of events, almost invariably arrived too late to be applicable to existing circumstances. To each marshal was assigned a distinct sphere of action ; and as they viewed each other with considerable jealousy, they very rarely co-operated at the proper time or in the proper direction. Even when they attempted to do so they were liable to be reprimanded by Napoleon, who, for example, when

Marmont proposed to assist Soult in the defence of Badajoz, told the former that "he was meddling with matters that did not concern him," and that " Badajoz was not committed to his charge." The King, with Marshal Jourdan as his chief of the staff, was given a nominal control over the commanders of the several French armies ; but these commanders reported to Napoleon direct, and continually disregarded Joseph's instructions. Without a supreme head present on the spot, whether that head be a commander-in-chief like Wellington, or a chief of the staff nominally subordinate to a royal personage like Von Moltke, it is impossible that military operations on an extended scale can be conducted with the unity of purpose and continuity of action which are essential to success ; and on this account the diffusion of responsibility and authority which Napoleon permitted and encouraged did much to neutralise the great numerical superiority of the French troops employed in the Peninsula.

A further point to be noticed is the extraordinary diplomatic skill which Wellington displayed in dealing with the Portuguese and Spanish authorities. They disliked him, but they feared him ; and by keeping his own counsel, and setting one party against another, he managed to get his own way without seeming unduly to interfere with the civil government. Here his Indian training was of great service. Brialmont observes: "Wellington's long experience of Indian intrigue gave him peculiar facilities for counteracting the selfish and shifting policy of the Peninsular nations; while his active participation in the government of Mysore had developed, to a great degree, the ability which was natural to him in the administration of political and civil offices. A leader deficient in these qualities would probably have failed in Spain, however great in other respects his military talent might have been."

Finally, Wellington's industry was indefatigable; and if genius is correctly described as being an infinite capacity for taking pains, he had every right to lay claim to that gift. Whatever matter came under his consideration, whether military, political, or financial, he dealt with it promptly and exhaustively. His correspondence alone would have taken up the whole time of any ordinary man, and in addition he had his own responsible duties as a commander-in-chief in the field to attend to. Moreover, he had only one or two generals under him on whom he could rely to carry out his instructions without his own personal supervision; and he was often obliged himself to undertake the duties of subordinate officers, to whom, in spite of his repeated remonstrances, leave of absence had been granted by the Horse Guards. In a letter to Lord Liverpool he remarked, " I am obliged to be everywhere, and, if absent from any operation, something goes wrong." And in another letter he informed the same Secretary of State that "the consequence of the absence of some of the general officers has been that in the late operations I have been obliged to be general of cavalry and of the advanced guard, and the leader of two or three columns, sometimes on the same day." The spirit which actuated Wellington is perhaps best described in his own words : " I work as hard as I can in every way in order to succeed."

There is one feature in Wellington's character which to some extent diminishes our admiration for his great qualities as a military commander. He was wanting in sympathy, and inclined to speak harshly and ungenerously of the officers and men who served under him during the Peninsular War. After capturing Oporto, he wrote : " I have long been of opinion that a British army could bear neither success nor failure." And again : " The army behave terribly ill. They are a rabble who cannot bear success any more than Sir John Moore's army could bear failure. I am endeavouring to tame them ; but if I should not succeed, I must make an official complaint of them, and send one or two corps home in disgrace." After the battle of Vittoria he addressed the Secretary of State as follows: "It is quite impossible for me or any other man to command a British army under the existing system. We have in the service the scum of the earth as common soldiers; and of late years we have been doing everything in our power to relax the discipline by which alone such men can be kept in order. The non-commissioned officers are as bad as the men. It is really a disgrace to have anything to say to such men as some of our soldiers are." Again he remarked: "We shall do no good until we change our system so far as to compel all ranks to do their duty." Again: "The ignorance of their duty of the officers of the army who are every day arriving in this country, and the general inattention and disobedience to orders by many of those who have been long here, increase the details of the duty to such an extent as to render it almost impracticable to carry it on; and, owing to this disobedience and neglect, I can depend upon nothing, however well regulated and ordered." Again: "Nobody in the British army ever reads an order as if it were to be a guide for his conduct, or in any other manner than as an amusing novel; and the consequence is that, when complicated arrangements are to be carried into execution, every gentleman proceeds according to his fancy ; and then, when it is found that the arrangement fails, they come upon me to set matters to rights, and thus my labour is increased tenfold." Once more : " The fact is that, if discipline means habits of obedience to orders as well as military instruction, we have but little of it in this army. Nobody ever thinks of obeying an order, and all the regulations of the Horse Guards, as well as of the War Office, and all the orders of the army applicable to this peculiar service, are so much waste-paper."

These strictures may have been natural and excusable at the time they were written, but, published as they were with Wellington's approval twenty-three years after the close of the war, they seem rather exaggerated and ungracious, especially when it is remembered that he used to declare that with such an army as he led in the Peninsula he could go anywhere and do anything, that he eulogised the *uniform* discipline, good conduct and gallantry of the officers and men in his farewell order of April 21st, 1814, and that to their exertions and sacrifices he owed his fame and fortune.

It is curious to contrast Napier's opinion of the British soldiers who served in the Peninsula with

Wellington's description of them as being " a rabble "
and "the scum of the earth."   In the second volume
of his history Napier says : " That the British infantry
soldier is more robust than the soldier of any other
nation can scarcely be doubted by those who, in 1815,
observed his powerful frame, distinguished amidst the
united armies of Europe ;   and, notwithstanding his
habitual excess in drinking, he sustains fatigue and
wet and the extremes of cold and heat with incredible
vigour.   When   completely   disciplined—and   three
years are required to accomplish this—his port is
lofty and his movements free, the whole world cannot
produce à nobler specimen of military bearing ; nor
is the mind unworthy of the outward man.   He does
not, indeed, possess that presumptuous vivacity which
would lead him to dictate to his commanders, or even
to censure real errors, although he may perceive
them ; but he is observant and quick to comprehend
his orders, full of resources under difficulties, calm
and resolute in danger, and more than usually
obedient and careful of his officers in moments of
imminent peril.   It has been asserted that his un-
deniable firmness in battle is the result of a phleg-
matic constitution uninspired by moral feeling.
Never was a more stupid calumny uttered !   Napoleon's troops fought in bright fields where every

helmet caught some gleams of glory, but the British soldier conquered under the cold shade of aristocracy. No honours awaited his daring, no despatch gave his name to the applauses of his countrymen ; his life of danger and hardship was uncheered by hope, his death unnoticed. Did his heart sink therefore ? Did he not endure with surpassing fortitude the sorest of ills, sustain the most terrible assaults in battle unmoved, overthrow with incredible energy every opponent, and at all times prove that, while no physical military qualification was wanting, the fount of honour was also full and fresh within him ?" So far as my own experience goes, I have every reason to believe that Napier's estimate of the British soldier's character is more correct than Wellington's.

In bringing this present chapter to a close, I cannot do better than quote the description given by the French historian, M. Alphonse de Beauchamps, of the position which Wellington had achieved during the second phase of his military career: "Napoleon mistook his destiny in not condescending to command in person the expedition of 1810. He did not perceive that he was winking at the inordinate growth of a name that Europe would soon be tempted to oppose to his own. Europe had plenty of soldiers to fight him. What it wanted was a man. After

Europe had seen the most illustrious marshals of the empire foiled by Wellington, it began to suspect that it had found what it sought. Napoleon had at length a rival."

WELLINGTON

"Nullum numen habes, si sit prudentia ; nos te
Nos facimus, Fortuna, deam, cœloque locamus."

CHAPTER III.

THE abdication of Napoleon, followed by the
restoration of the Bourbon dynasty, ended the war
between France and the Allied Powers ; the Peninsular Army was broken up, and Wellington returned
to England after having visited Paris and Madrid.
At the latter place he was well received by King
Ferdinand, on whom he urged the expediency of
adopting a moderate and constitutional course in
dealing with the Spanish people. He reached
London on June 23rd, 1814, and was enthusiastically
welcomed by all classes of the British public. On
July 5th he was appointed Ambassador to the Court
of France, and left England early in August to take
up his duties. But before entering upon them he was
instructed to examine personally the Belgian frontier,
and to report on the most suitable measures for put-

ting it in a state of defence. The British Government thought it desirable to obtain the Duke of Wellington's opinion on this question, as the Kingdom of the Netherlands had just been established by European agreement to serve as a bulwark against French aggression, and a force composed of British, Hanoverian, Dutch, and Belgian troops was then occupying the country. In preparing his report the Duke was assisted by several experienced officers of the Royal Engineers ; and, after a careful reconnaissance, he arrived at the conclusion that the frontier was so accessible to an invader, so intersected by roads, canals and rivers, and so devoid of the natural obstacles which might be expected to restrict an enemy's operations, that it would be impossible to protect it by means of a single powerful fortress. He recommended, therefore, that the *cordon* of fortifications and dikes, which had been originally constructed under Austrian rule, should be put in order and improved ; and he further pointed out certain positions which might advantageously be occupied by a field army resisting a French invasion. He showed his military acumen by selecting as one of these positions the actual site on which the battle of Waterloo was fought in the following year.

This duty being completed, Wellington proceeded

ENGLAND'S HOPE, 1815.

From O'Connor Morris's "Great Commanders."

To face p. 128.

to Paris, where he arrived on August 22nd. He
was received with a fair show of cordiality by
Louis XVIII. and his ministers, but in a less friendly
spirit by the Court party and a section of the Bona-
partists. His tenure of the appointment only lasted
for about five months, during which no really important diplomatic questions came under consideration. At that time a strong feeling prevailed in
England in favour of the immediate abolition of the
slave trade, and Wellington was directed to use every
means in his power to obtain the active support and
co-operation of the French Government. The French
people, however, though the advocates of universal
freedom in the abstract, were hardly prepared to
accept the views held by Mr. Wilberforce and other
prominent abolitionists unless they obtained some
compensating advantage ; and a hint was thrown out
that the cession by England of one of the more
important West Indian Islands, such as Trinidad,
might materially facilitate the progress of the
negotiations. This proposal did not find favour with
the British ministry, and was not seriously pressed.
The question remained still undecided when Lord
Castlereagh, who, as Secretary of State for Foreign
Affairs, was representing Great Britain at the Congress of Vienna, found it necessary to return to his

parliamentary duties, and Wellington was chosen to
replace him.   Leaving Paris towards the end of
January 1815, the Duke reached Vienna early in
February, and there found the several European
Powers quarrelling amongst themselves about the
redistribution of the territory set free by Napoleon's
abdication.   The existing state of affairs was unsettled
and complicated.   As already mentioned, a joint
army of occupation commanded by the Prince of
Orange was quartered in the Low Countries, while
the German provinces on the right bank of the Meuse,
extending from Lorraine to the junction of the
Meuse and Rhine, were held by a Prussian force.   In
compensation for her efforts to overthrow Napoleon,
Russia laid claim to the whole of Poland, and Prussia
was resolved to annex the entire kingdom of Saxony.
These demands were resisted by England and Austria,
as being contrary to the wish of the populations
concerned, and likely to upset the European equili-
brium ; and the objections raised to the undue
aggrandisement of the two northern Powers were
supported by the representative of the French
Government.   The Emperor Alexander was so much
irritated at this opposition that he encouraged Murat,
who had been allowed to retain the Neapolitan throne,
to occupy a portion of the Papal States, and largely

to increase his army as a menace to Austria and France. Austria accordingly concentrated 150,000 men in Northern Italy, the Russian troops which were returning to their own country were halted in Poland, and Prussia declared her determination to keep Saxony by force of arms. A secret treaty was entered into by Austria, France and England, and a general European war seemed far from improbable.

The aspect of affairs, however, was suddenly changed by news received on March 7th that Napoleon had escaped from Elba ; and the sovereigns and statesmen assembled at Vienna had to abandon their mutual animosities in order to face a common danger. A few days afterwards a report was received that the Emperor had landed in France with only a thousand men at his command, and was marching upon Paris. At first it was thought that the French troops would remain faithful to the Bourbon dynasty, and that Napoleon's enterprise would fail. Louis XVIII. assured the Ambassadors at his Court that there was no reason for alarm. Marshal Soult, who had been appointed War Minister, issued an order of the day in which he congratulated the army on having at its head the Comte d'Artois, whom he described as "the model of French chivalry." He added : "Bonaparte mistakes us so far as to believe that we are capable of abandoning a legitimate and beloved sovereign in order to share the fortunes of one who is nothing more than an adventurer. He believes this—the idiot!—and his last act of folly is a convincing proof that he does so." Marshel Ney was directed by the King to meet and arrest the Emperor. "Go," said Louis XVIII. to him : "I trust to your fidelity and devotion." Ney promised, in reply, that he would bring back the usurper in an iron cage. He had not proceeded far when his sentiments changed. He remarked : "What would you have me do ? I cannot stop the waters of the sea with my hand." And shortly afterwards, forming up his troops, he read to them Napoleon's proclamation, and issued an order of the day beginning—"Soldiers, the cause of the Bourbons is lost for ever." On March 20th Napoleon entered Paris, and Louis XVIII., with his Court, fled across the Belgian frontier.

At this crisis England and the Continental Powers were united in their determination to prevent Napoleon from re-establishing himself as the ruler of France, although before leaving Elba he had caused it to be made known that he was prepared to adhere to the Treaty of Paris, and would in future confine himself to the internal administration of his own country. As usual, the first thought of England's Continental allies was to extract liberal subsidies from the British Government. After the Peace of Tilsit Russia had endeavoured to persuade the French Emperor to join her in an attack on our Eastern possessions. She had encouraged him in his attempt to subjugate Spain and Portugal. Her whole policy had been to intensify the ill-feeling between France and England, in order to distract attention from her own aggressive designs in Europe and Asia. It is therefore a remarkable illustration of Russian assurance to find that in 1815 the Tsar was particularly pressing and persistent in his demands for pecuniary assistance; and it is an equally remarkable illustration of the somewhat indiscriminate generosity of British statesmen to find that the Tsar's demands, in common with those of the other sovereigns, were complied with to an extent which seems to have rendered England the general paymaster of the Allied Forces. So far, indeed, was this generosity carried that the British Government actually agreed to pay the expenses of the French mission at the Vienna Congress.

On March 13th the Congress of Vienna issued a declaration placing Napóleon *hors des relations civiles et sociales*, and on the 25th of the same month a formal treaty was concluded providing for the concentration of an overwhelming force on the French frontier. The following scheme of mobilisation was decided on:—The troops of the United Kingdom, Hanover, Brunswick, and the Netherlands were to occupy Belgium under Wellington's command. The Prussian army under Marshal Blucher was to take up its position between the Rhine and the Meuse. The contingents from Bavaria, Wurtemberg, and Baden were to assemble in the Black Forest and Palatinate, and there to be joined by an Austrian force, the command of the whole being assumed by Marshal Schwarzenberg. The Russian army, marching from Poland through Germany, was to form upon the Rhine, the Main, and the Moselle.

Wellington left Vienna on March 29th, and reached Brussels on April 5th, where he relieved the Prince of Orange of the command of the troops quartered in the Low Countries. He was at first inclined to underrate the strength and mobility of the force at Napoleon's disposal, and he drew up a memorandum, dated April 12th, advocating an advance of the Allied armies into France by May 1st. The more accurate information which he subsequently received led him to modify his original estimate of the enemy's resources ; and, besides, he found his own army so weak and badly equipped, and composed of soldiers differing so much in quality and nationality,

that it was absolutely necessary to await reinforcements and supplies, and to make a careful distribution
of the good and inferior troops so as to render the
whole force as uniformly efficient as possible. He
thought it desirable also to improvise such fortifications along the Belgian frontier as would impede the
enemy's advance and facilitate his own movements.
And last, but not least, he ascertained that considerable delay was likely to occur in the arrival of the
Austrian and Russian corps on the French frontier.

Writing to Lord Bathurst on May 2nd, the Duke
expressed the opinion that, if Napoleon decided to act
on the offensive, he would probably begin by attacking
the Bavarians, who, to the number of 25,000, had
crossed the Rhine and taken up a position in the
vicinity of Germersheim. On May 8th he seems to
have regarded it as not unlikely that Napoleon would
act on the defensive and await the invasion of the
Allied armies. In that case he considered the difficulties in the way of an advance upon Paris from the
Belgian frontier to be so formidable, that he doubted
whether his own force, in combination with the
Prussian army under Blucher, could move until the
troops assembled on the upper Rhine under Schwarzenberg had begun their forward movement and had
thus obliged the French Emperor to concentrate upon

the Aisne. On May 9th he addressed the Duc de Berri in the following terms : " J'avoue à votre Altesse Royale que j'ai toute raison de croire la force ennemie à présent rassemblée à Valenciennes et Maubeuge très supérieure à ce qu'elle a été représentée à votre Altesse ; et que je ne serais pas surpris que nous fussions attaqués." The same day he used similar language in writing to Lord Hill. Three days afterwards he wrote as follows to his brother Henry : " There has been a good deal of movement upon the frontier in the last week, but I am inclined to believe it is entirely defensive, and that Bonaparte cannot venture to quit Paris. Indeed, all accounts give reason to hope that, even without the aid of the Allies, *his* power will not be of long duration." In a memorandum written in 1842, controverting certain statements which had appeared in General Clausewitz's history of the campaign of 1815, Wellington explained the exact position occupied by the British and Prussian forces, and the alternative lines of action for which they had to be prepared. He pointed out that the two Allied armies guarding the Belgian frontier were "necessarily on the defensive, waiting for the junction of other large armies, to attain, by their co-operation, a common object ;" but that "their defensive position and immediate objects did not necessarily preclude all idea or plan of attack upon the enemy." Such ideas or plans had, however, to be postponed because Napoleon took up a position "in which his numbers, his movements and his designs could be concealed, protected, and supported by his formidable fortresses on the frontier, up to the last moment previous to their being carried into execution. The initiative, then, rested with the enemy ; and the course to be pursued by the Allied generals respectively was to be prepared to move in all directions, to wait till it should be seen in what direction the attack would be made, and then to assemble the armies as quickly as possible to resist the attack, or to attack the enemy with the largest force that could be collected." He emphasised the necessity for extreme watchfulness and caution by observing that, whatever might be thought of Napoleon as a leader of troops in other respects, "there certainly never existed a man in whose presence it was so little safe to make what is called a false movement."

I have referred in some detail to the somewhat inconsistent views put forward by Wellington in regard to the nature and direction of Napoleon's operations, in order to show how difficult it is for even the most sagacious and experienced commander to fathom the designs of an equally able antagonist.

But, whatever schemes he might elaborate for the eventual invasion of France, the Duke did not neglect his more immediate duty, which was to arrange for the rapid concentration of his army at any threatened point, and to improve his own defensive position. On April 30th he circulated a secret memorandum giving specific instructions to his subordinate commanders for the movement of the troops under their orders, in the event of a French attack between the Lys and Scheldt, or between the Sambre and Scheldt, or by both lines simultaneously. He caused the fortifications of Ypres, Ostend, Nieuport, Ath, and Tournay to be repaired and armed. Mons was protected by inundations and redoubts. The defences of Antwerp were strengthened, and Ghent was covered by a line of field works extending from the Lys to the Scheldt. Audenarde also was fortified, in order to facilitate the movement of troops along either bank of the latter river. Writing to the Prince of Orange on April 17th, Wellington pointed out that the King of the Netherlands "had but a small and very young army to oppose to the well-disciplined French troops," and that the inhabitants of Belgium were not particularly well disposed towards the existing Government. Under these circumstances he was of opinion that the most useful way to employ such an army was to place it in well-chosen works of defence. Subsequently garrisons were allotted to the several places mentioned above, consisting of about 2000 British troops, 10,000 Hanoverians, and 14,000 soldiers of the Low Countries. As explained by Colonel Carmichael Smyth, the Commanding Royal Engineer, " the object of these various works was not to stop the French from invading Belgium, but to detain them long enough to give the Allies time to concentrate upon their line of operations." That this object was attained is evident from Wellington's account of the concentration on Quatre Bras during the evening and night of June 15th, his words being—" The whole army moved on that evening and in the night, each division and portion separately ; the whole being protected on the march by the defensive works constructed at the different points referred to, and by their garrisons."

As regards the army placed under his command, Wellington, on arriving at Brussels, expressed his dissatisfaction at the inadequate number of British troops despatched to the Low Countries. He remarked to Lord Bathurst that the Home Government had not taken a clear view of the situation, and that, if the war was to be a short one, a great effort was necessary. He asked for 40,000 good British infantry

in addition to the number required for garrisons,
18,000 cavalry, and 150 field guns manned by British
artillerymen and fully horsed. He also requested
that the entire corps of Sappers and Miners should be
sent to the scene of operations, as well as a bridge
train of eighty pontoons, a waggon train, ambulance
corps, and proper transport for small arms ammunition. With these equipments and reinforcements he
engaged that the British army would creditably play
its part in the game ; but added, "As it is, we are in
a bad way." Writing to General Lord Stewart, on
May 8th, he expressed himself as follows : "I have
got an infamous army, very weak and ill-equipped,
and a very inexperienced staff. In my opinion they
are doing nothing in England. They have not raised
a man ; they have not called out the militia either in
England or Ireland ; are unable to send me anything ;
and they have not sent a message to Parliament
about the money." The Duke strongly objected to
the excessive number of general and staff officers
appointed to the force by the Horse Guards, and to
the selection of officers who were absolutely ignorant
of their staff duties. Writing to the Military Secretary, he observed : "The army—that is, the British
part of it—is excessively small, and it already has a
staff more than sufficient for its numbers and organ-

isation. . . . I am certain that His Royal Highness would wish to nominate the staff officers most capable of serving the army and those about whom they are placed ; and he will admit that the most experienced —that is, those that have been serving in staff situations for five or six years—are of that description. But of the list you and Colonel Shawe have sent, there are only three who have any experience at all. As for the others, if they had been proposed to me, I should have rejected them all." He wrote again on the same day, "Before you send any more general officers let me see more troops." Finding that his remonstrances were not well received by His Royal Highness, Wellington thought it better to give way, and informed the Military Secretary that he would not object to having as many officers on the staff as the Commander-in-Chief chose to nominate. But he pointed out that the staff was to a great extent useless. Speaking of the departments of Military Intelligence and Military Communications, he remarked : "It is quite impossible for me to superintend the details of the duties of these departments myself, having already more to arrange than I am equal to, and I cannot entrust them to the young gentlemen on the staff of this army. Indeed, I must say I do not know how to employ them." And he finally wrote, on May 5th: " I think it much better that this correspondence upon the Staff should cease. The Commander-in-Chief has a right to appoint whom he chooses, and those whom he appoints shall be employed. It cannot be expected that I should declare

H.R.H. FREDERICK, DUKE OF YORK AND ALBANY, F.-M., COMMANDER-IN-CHIEF.

myself satisfied with these appointments till I shall find the persons as fit for their situations as those whom I should have recommended to His Royal Highness."

Wellington, as we know, had a high opinion of the

Portuguese troops, when led by British officers and associated with British soldiers. He endeavoured, therefore, to strengthen his army by obtaining from Portugal a contingent of 15,000 picked men under the command of Marshal Beresford. He addressed the Prince Regent of Portugal on the subject, and also submitted repeated applications to the Home Government. No objection was raised by the authorities concerned ; the force, with artillery and baggage-train, was assembled, and the transports were ready for its embarkation. But unfortunately Canning, who was then Ambassador at Lisbon, determined to proceed by strictly diplomatic methods, the Souza faction took advantage of the opportunity to oppose the despatch of the contingent, and the army of England's traditional ally lost its chance of sharing in the glories of the campaign of 1815.

Turning now to the state of affairs at the beginning of June, we find that the Allied troops under Wellington's command were holding the fortified posts along the Belgian frontier from Ostend to Mons. The right wing, under General Hill, was stationed in the neighbourhood of Ath, and the left wing, under the Prince of Orange, occupied Braine-le-Comte and Nivelles. The cavalry, commanded by Lord Uxbridge, was collected at Grammont, and the

reserve of all arms was encamped and cantoned at
Brussels, which place was also the Duke's headquarters.   The troops of all ranks numbered altogether about 110,000, of whom a little over 49,000
(including the King's German Legion) were British,
and the remainder Hanoverians, Brunswickers, Dutch-
men, and Belgians.   Out of this total some 20,000
men were employed in garrisoning Antwerp, Ostend,
Nieuport, and the frontier defences, leaving a field army
about 90,000 strong, with 200 guns.   Blucher's army,
consisting of four corps and numbering 117,000 men,
with 300 guns, was quartered at Charleroi, Namur,
Dinant and Liége.   At the same date the force at
Napoleon's disposal amounted to about 128,000 men,
with 350 guns, and occupied cantonments facing the
Belgian frontier, from Lille on the left to Metz on
the right.   In addition, there were some 53,000
regular troops doing duty in garrisons and as corps
of observation in various parts of France.

There were three courses open to the French
Emperor.   He might have endeavoured to negotiate
with the Allied Powers ; but such an attempt seemed
useless—at any rate until he had gained a decisive
victory—in view of the declaration placing him *hors
de la loi*, and the treaty binding the Powers to continue the struggle until he was driven from the

French throne. Secondly, he might have maintained a defensive attitude, and awaited the attack of the Allies along a front stretching from Paris to Lyons. But to do this would have been to diminish his resources by abandoning a large portion of France to

FIELD-MARSHAL VON BLUCHER.

the enemy, to alienate the population of the invaded provinces, and to dishearten his own troops. The third course was to attack and defeat the Anglo-Prussian force before the Austrian and Russian corps had time to concentrate on the French frontier. It

L

is true that the French army was numerically much
weaker than the combined armies of England and
Prussia.   But Napoleon's previous successes had
induced him to believe that this inequality would be
more than counterbalanced by his skill as a general,
and by the superiority of his soldiers.   Besides, he
considered, to use his own words, that " an offensive
plan of action was alone in conformity with the genius
of the French nation and with the spirit and principles of the war in which he was engaged."   He
hoped to take the Allies by surprise, to beat them in
detail before they could unite, and to bring about a
national rising in Belgium and the Rhine Provinces.
For these reasons the third course commended
itself to the Emperor, as offering him the best, if not
the only, chance of success.

Having determined to assume the offensive, Napoleon decided to operate by the valley of the Sambre,
and strike at the point of junction between the
British and Prussian forces.   The long front occupied
by the Allies was exposed to attack in other directions ; and he might have advanced by the Meuse
valley with the object of cutting off the Prussians
from their base at Cologne, or he might have endeavoured to turn the right flank of Wellington's
army, driving it back in an eastward direction and

threatening its communications with the sea, Holland, and Hanover. In adopting the central line of operations, it seems probable that Napoleon failed to realise what an able and active enemy he had to deal with; for it is obvious that, unless he could effectually interpose between the British and Prussian armies before they had time to concentrate on their point of junction, he ran the risk of being attacked by them simultaneously. Even if he were fortunate enough to defeat and drive back one of these armies, the other army might prevent him from following up his success by menacing his flank and rear; while if, under the same circumstances, he proceeded to attack the force which had not yet been engaged, the defeated army might come to its ally's assistance—unless, indeed, its defeat had been so disastrous as to render it incapable for the time of further interference with his movements. Wellington was always of opinion that the French Emperor would have done better if he had selected another line of operations, and the result of the campaign to a great extent confirms the correctness of this view.

The concentration of the French army was carried out with the precision and secrecy characteristic of Napoleon's strategy, and by June 14th his force was assembled upon the line stretching from Maubeuge

through Beaumont to Philippeville, within one march
of Charleroi, which was held by Ziethen's corps of
30,000 Prussians. Early the next day the French
troops came into contact with the Prussian outposts,
and crossed the Sambre at Charleroi, Marchiennes,
and Chatelet, Ziethen's corps falling back in good
order first on Fleurus and afterwards on Ligny.
Blucher received the news of Napoleon's advance on
the 14th, and at once gave orders for the concentration of his army at Fleurus. The same intelligence
was first communicated to Wellington at three o'clock
in the afternoon of the 15th by the Prince of Orange,
whose report was shortly afterwards confirmed by
General Muffling, the Prussian Staff Officer at the
Duke's headquarters. Orders were issued forthwith
for the British army to be prepared to concentrate on
its left at a moment's notice, but for some little time
Wellington doubted whether Napoleon had really
committed himself to an attack upon the centre of
the position occupied by the Allied forces. The
news received in the afternoon was, however, sub-
stantiated a few hours later, and at 10 P.M. the troops
were directed to move upon Quatre Bras. The
reserve quartered in and near Brussels was assembled
on the evening of the 15th, and began its march to
Quatre Bras at daybreak on the 16th.

On the morning of the 16th Ziethen's corps was at
Ligny, about eight miles south-east of Quatre Bras.
It was there joined at an early hour by Pirch's corps,
32,000 strong, and Thielman's, 21,000 strong, the
whole being under Blucher's personal command.
Bulow's corps, numbering 30,000, which had been
quartered at Liége, some fifty miles distant, did not
come up in time to take part in the operations of the
day. A division of the troops of the Netherlands
about 10,000 strong, commanded by the Prince of
Orange, was holding Quatre Bras and awaiting the
arrival of the reinforcements which had been ordered
up at 10 o'clock the preceding evening. Wellington
left Brussels early in the morning, after having
attended with many of his officers the famous ball
given by the Duchess of Richmond. He reached
Quatre Bras about 10 A.M., reconnoitred the French
troops which had halted in front of the Prince of
Orange's division, and rode on to Ligny, where he had
an interview with the Prussian Commander-in-Chief.
He is said to have disapproved of the position which
Blucher had taken up between St. Amand and
Sombreffe, telling the Marshal—"Every man knows
his own troops best ; but if I were to place my men
where you have placed yours, I should expect to
be beaten." Blucher's reply was—"My men like to

see the enemy"; and the Duke did not continue the discussion. But when riding back to Quatre Bras he remarked to his staff—"If I am not very much mistaken, the Prussians will get an awful thrashing to-day."

Wellington got back to Quatre Bras between 3 and 4 P.M. He tells us that the reserve from Brussels had arrived there about noon, and was shortly afterwards followed by the Brunswick and Nassau contingents, 1st Infantry Division consisting of the Foot Guards, and a portion of the Cavalry and Artillery. It is only fair to say that, though the Duke's statement on this point in his memorandum on Clausewitz's history is quite clear, he reported in his official despatch that the reserve only reached Quatre Bras at half-past two in the afternoon ; and other authorities assert that the Prince of Orange was not reinforced until four o'clock, and that the British cavalry and artillery did not come up until six o'clock.

Napoleon's plans for the 16th were as follows :—He assumed the personal command of the right and centre of his army, consisting of about 73,000 men, with 230 guns ; and the command of the left, consisting of some 47,000 men, with 120 guns, was given to Marshal Ney, who had arrived from Paris late in the evening of the preceding day. Ney's headquarters

were at Gosselies, about eight miles south of Quatre
Bras, and there he received a letter dictated by the
Emperor at 8 A.M., desiring him to occupy the position
held by the Prince of Orange, and afterwards to be
in readiness for a rapid march on Brussels. The instructions given in this letter were singularly vague,
and indicated a misapprehension of the true state of
affairs. Napoleon wrote : " I shall attack the enemy
if I fall in with them. Then, after the engagement
is over, I shall begin my march at three in the afternoon—perhaps in the evening. My wish is for you
to be ready to move immediately after I have started.
I desire you to make such arrangements as will enable
your eight divisions, on the receipt of orders from me,
to march rapidly and without check upon Brussels."
Napoleon evidently looked upon victory as assured.

The Emperor reached Fleurus at about 11 A.M.,
and personally reconnoitred Blucher's position. The
information he obtained seems to have been very
imperfect, for shortly afterwards, Soult, who was
Chief of the Staff, wrote to Ney in the following
terms : " The Emperor commands me to inform you
that the enemy has collected a body of troops between
Bry and Sombreffe ; and that at half-past two Marshal
Grouchy, with the 3rd and 4th Corps, will fall upon
him." The body of troops thus referred to was in

reality the Prussian army, over 80,000 strong, drawn
up in readiness to oppose Napoleon's advance. It had
been the Emperor's intention to take the Allied forces
by surprise. He appears to have taken it for granted
that he had succeeded in doing so, and he apprehended
no serious opposition to his preventing their junction.
That junction, however, had actually been effected
about midday, although Napoleon remained ignorant
of the fact until his dispositions had been made, and
his troops were engaged.

Ney began his attack on Quatre Bras at 2 P.M., and
Napoleon engaged the Prussian troops about half an
hour later. The resistance of the latter was so
obstinate, and their strength so much greater than the
Emperor had anticipated, that shortly after three
o'clock, he sent an order to Ney directing him to
manœuvre in the direction of Bry, so as to turn the
Prussian right. As this order was being conveyed
to Ney, it was shown to Marshal D'Erlon, one of
his commanders, who, with a corps of 20,000 men,
and forty-six guns, was moving up in support of
the attack on Quatre Bras. Without waiting for
instructions from his immediate superior, D'Erlon
decided to comply with the order, and accordingly
turned off in the direction of Bry, which he reached
about 7 P.M. Meanwhile, Ney was being pushed back

by Wellington, and finding himself in urgent need of reinforcements he sent peremptory orders to D'Erlon to retrace his steps towards Quatre Bras. The result was that on June 17th, an entire corps with forty-six guns spent the day in marching to and fro between the left and centre of the French army.

After a severe and protracted struggle, the Prussians, as predicted by Wellington, were defeated, but not routed, at Ligny, while the English were victorious at Quatre Bras, driving the French back to Frasnes, and themselves bivouacking on the field of battle. During these engagements, both Wellington and Blucher narrowly escaped being killed or captured by the enemy.* During the night the Prussian force drew off

---

* Blucher placed himself at the head of a body of Prussian cavalry, and charged the French squadrons which were pursuing his defeated infantry. His horse was shot under him, and entangled him in his fall; and he lay, fortunately unrecognised, on the field of battle until his aide-de-camp was able to remount him on a charger taken from one of his own troopers.

At Quatre Bras Wellington accompanied a regiment of Brunswicker Hussars, which he had ordered up in support of the infantry of the same contingent. This regiment was composed of young soldiers, and being exposed to a hot musketry fire, it fell back in confusion. The Duke was carried away with it, and, the French Lancers charging at the moment, he had to trust to the speed of his horse. He arrived, closely pursued, at the edge of a ditch which was lined by the 92nd Highlanders, and, leaping his horse across the ditch and over the Highlanders' bayonets, he drew up in safety on the other

in the direction of Wavre, their retirement being conducted in such a leisurely manner, that on the morning
of the 17th, their rear-guard was still at Sombreffe.
Shortly after daybreak, Wellington communicated
with General Ziethen, commanding the rear-guard,
through Colonel Gordon, one of his aides-de-camp,
whose escort, consisting of two squadrons of the 10th
Hussars, drove in the French vedettes posted on the
field of Ligny.

About 8 A.M. on the 17th, Napoleon proceeded to
St. Amand and spent three or four hours in inspecting
his troops, and visiting the scene of the previous day's
conflict with the Prussians.   He assumed that the
latter had withdrawn eastward towards their base in
Germany, but took no steps to verify the accuracy of
this conjecture.   He accordingly placed Grouchy in
command of about 33,000 men with ninety-six guns,
and directed him to pursue the Prussians through
Gembloux in the direction of Namur and Liége.
This order, which was a verbal one, was not given
until early in the afternoon. It was followed by written
instructions to the same effect ; and after an unnecessary delay of at least eight hours, for which the

---

side. A French officer, named Burgoyne, made a dash at the
Duke, but was stopped by a musket-ball from one of the 92nd,
which passed through both his ankles.

Emperor alone was responsible, Grouchy began his march at 3 P.M. in a wrong direction.

In the meantime, ascertaining that the English were still holding Quatre Bras, the Emperor wrote to Ney a letter dated "Noon, in front of Ligny," desiring him to engage the enemy, and promising him to support the attack by an advance upon Marbais. Wellington's main body had, however, fallen back about 10 A.M. without interruption or molestation towards the position he had selected in front of Waterloo, and only the outposts and cavalry remained at Quatre Bras, under his personal command. His own account is: "No pursuit was made of the Prussian army, or movement of any kind made by the French army, until a late hour in the afternoon of the 17th. The largest body of French troops and the great mass of the cavalry moved down the high road from Sombreffe to Quatre Bras, towards the left of the British troops of the army of the Duke of Wellington, which still remained on that ground. These were put in motion, and retired as soon as their outposts were touched by the enemy, and joined the main body of the army at that time posted in front of Waterloo." So far, then, Napoleon had gained no material advantage. He had failed to anticipate the concentration, or to prevent the

junction, of the Allied forces opposed to him ; he had
fought a double engagement without decisive results ;
Blucher, having been defeated, had fallen back in
good order on Wavre ; and Wellington, having
gained the day at Quatre Bras, had withdrawn to a
position which offered great defensive advantages
besides being within easy reach of the Prussian force.

At nightfall the main body of the French army,
numbering 72,000 men with 240 guns, was collected
within a mile of the troops under Wellington's
command ; but Grouchy's corps, which had been
detached in pursuit of the Prussians, had started at so
late an hour that by nine in the evening it had only
advanced as far as Gembloux, about fourteen miles
from Wavre and twenty miles from Waterloo. On
reaching Gembloux, Grouchy ascertained that a
considerable portion of the Prussian force had retreated towards Wavre, and he reported to Napoleon
accordingly, proposing to continue his pursuit in that
direction early next morning. This course of action
was approved by the Emperor, but the French
troops did not quit Gembloux until about 9 A.M. on
the 18th, and it was only at 11 A.M., when passing
through Sart-lez-Walhain, that Grouchy became
aware of the concentration of the whole Prussian
army at Wavre on the previous night. The heavy

rain which fell during the afternoon and night of the
17th somewhat modified the operations of the
following day, though it can hardly be said to have
affected their result. In the first place, the state of
the roads greatly delayed the movement of the
Prussians in support of Wellington's left, while it
retarded to an equal extent Grouchy's march from
Gembloux to Wavre; and, secondly, the ground at
Waterloo had become so heavy that Napoleon decided not to begin the battle until 11 A.M., by which
time he expected to be able to manœuvre his cavalry
and artillery. The first phase of the engagement
was an attack on the British right at the advanced
post of Hougoumont, a building surrounded by
orchards and enclosures, and occupied by a detachment of the Guards. The building itself was set on
fire by the French shells, and the enclosures .sur-
rounding it fell for a time into the enemy's hands;
but eventually the assailants were repulsed, and the
defenders held their ground up to the close of the
day. This attempt to turn the British right proving
unsuccessful, D'Erlon's corps, 20,000 strong, was
directed against the British left centre at about half-
past one in the afternoon. Moving in four dense
columns, the French infantry quickly routed a brigade
of Belgian troops which obstructed their advance;

Burying Ground
Farms
Infantry
Cavalry
Cannon
British
Prussians
Belgians
French

THE FIELD OF WATERLOO.

but coming next into contact with Picton's division, drawn up in rear of the Belgians, they recoiled in disorder before its deadly fire. The brigade of heavy cavalry under Ponsonby seized the opportunity to charge the wavering masses of the enemy, driving them back in the utmost confusion, and capturing 3000 prisoners. The cavalry continued their pursuit as far as the batteries which had been supporting D'Erlon's attack; but, after sabring many horses and upsetting fifteen guns, they were charged in turn by the French squadrons, and had to retire with heavy loss, their gallant commander being among the killed. About 3 P.M. Ney again attacked the British left centre, and succeeded in gaining possession of a farmhouse called La Haye Sainte, which Wellington had occupied as a defensive outpost covering this flank of his position. An hour later the Duke attempted to recapture La Haye Sainte; but the Hanoverians, to whom the task was entrusted, were repulsed by the French troops, and a gap was thus made in the British line, through which Ney endeavoured to penetrate. Having no infantry immediately available for this purpose, he ordered up a brigade of cavalry, which, either accidentally or in accordance with the Emperor's instructions, was followed by the main body of that arm including

the reserve cavalry of the Imperial Guard. Wellington, however, brought up reinforcements ; and his
infantry, formed into squares, stubbornly resisted the
repeated charges of the French horsemen, who had at
last to fall back completely disorganised by the cool
and accurate fire of their opponents.

We must now turn to the Prussian army, which
on the night of the 17th had bivouacked in the
neighbourhood of Wavre. In order to appreciate
the plan of campaign of the Allied generals, it must
be remembered that throughout the operations
Wellington was in constant communication with
Blucher. As already mentioned, he had an interview
with the latter on the battle-field of Ligny. Early
the next morning he sent one of his aides-de-camp to
ascertain from General Ziethen the line of retreat of
the Prussian force to Wavre, and shortly afterwards
he received a despatch from Blucher conveyed by
Lieutenant Massow. He has himself stated that
the exact position of the Prussians and the intentions of their commander were known to him
before he broke up his own position at Quatre
Bras, and that "the two Allied armies communicated with each other throughout the night of
June 17th." Up to the battle of Ligny Wellington
and Blucher were kept in close touch with each

other's plans and movements through Colonel Sir
Henry Hardinge, the British Commissioner at the
Prussian headquarters, and General Müffling, the
Prussian Commissioner at the British headquarters.
Hardinge was severely wounded at Ligny, and for
the next few days General Müffling had to under-
take his colleague's duties in addition to his own.
Speaking of the latter officer, Wellington remarked :
" We were engaged in strict co-operation with the
Prussian army, and he necessarily carried on a very
active and almost hourly correspondence with the
Prussian headquarters, particularly after Hardinge
was wounded in the battle of Ligny." It may therefore be concluded that a clear understanding had
been come to between the Allied generals that the
British army should engage Napoleon in front of
Waterloo while Blucher attacked him on the right
flank from the direction of Wavre. Wavre is barely
ten miles from Waterloo, and two nearly parallel
roads connected the two places, one through Ohain
on Mont St. Jean, the other through St. Lambert to
Planchenois. In view of these facts it seems reasonable to assume that Wellington had arranged to be
supported by a strong body of Prussian troops not
later than one or two o'clock in the afternoon. At
daylight on the 18th the cavalry of General Bulow's

M

corps was visible on the high ground in front of
Ohain, less than four miles from the British position ;
but, owing to the bad state of the roads and several
accidental circumstances, it was two in the afternoon
before the infantry of that corps had passed through

THE MARQUESS OF ANGLESEY.

St. Lambert, and half-past four before the Prussians
deployed for attack in front of Planchenois. Napoleon
had detached General Lobau with 10,000 men to
meet this flanking movement ; but the French troops
were driven back into the village of Planchenois and

had to be reinforced an hour later by a division of
the Young Guard, a regiment of the Old Guard, and
twenty-four guns. At 7 P.M. Ziethen's corps, marching through Ohain, came up on the left of the British
line, and assisted in defeating the Emperor's final
attack. For this attack Napoleon formed eight
battalions of the Guard, hitherto held in reserve, into
two columns, two additional battalions following in
support. The columns were opposed by a line of
British infantry, consisting of Maitland's brigade of
the Foot Guards led by Wellington in person, and
they were taken in flank by the 52nd Regiment.
Being exposed to an overwhelming fire, to which,
from the nature of their formation, they were unable
to reply, they halted and wavered. At that moment
they were charged by two brigades of British cavalry,
and after a brief struggle driven back in disorder.
At this critical moment Ziethen's corps, led by
Blucher, engaged the French right and carried the
position it occupied at Papelotte and La Haye.
Seizing the opportunity, Wellington ordered a
general advance of his whole line of infantry, supported by his cavalry and artillery. To use his own
words, "the attack succeeded at every point; the
enemy was forced from his position on the heights,
and fled in the utmost confusion, leaving behind him,

as far as I could judge, 150 pieces of cannon, with
their ammunition, which fell into our hands."

The pursuit was begun by both British and Prussian
troops. The former, however, were much fatigued,
and both on this account and because there was not
room for them to act along the Charleroi road simultaneously with the Prussians, Wellington arranged
with Blucher that the latter should follow up the
enemy throughout the night. By daybreak the
next morning the Prussian cavalry had reached
Gosselies, about five miles short of Charleroi and
twenty miles from the battle-field; and had captured
sixty guns belonging to the Imperial Guard. The
Emperor passed through Charleroi at 6 A.M., and out
of the army 72,000 strong which he commanded at
Waterloo, only 40,000 recrossed the Sambre. The
total loss of the Allies on June 18th amounted to
over 23,000 killed and wounded, that of the British
being 8460, and of the Prussians 7000.

Here it should be mentioned that a portion of
Wellington's available force was not present on the
field of battle. One division under General Colville,
consisting of four British and five Hanoverian battalions, with three British batteries, was posted at
Hal, on the road between Mons and Brussels, while
a corps of Netherlanders, 17,000 strong, under Prince

Frederick of Orange, occupied the ground between Hal and Enghien. It has generally been supposed that these troops were detached with the object of guarding the right flank of the Duke's army against a turning movement. But it seems most unlikely that such a commander as Wellington was ignorant of the fact that the whole French army, except Grouchy's corps, had taken up its position immediately in front of him on the evening of the 17th ; and from some remarks of his, recorded by Mr. Gleig, it would appear that his intention in holding Hal and Enghien on the 18th was to secure his line of retreat in the event of his being defeated. In December, 1825, Wellington, in discussing with Mr. Croker the assertion made by Napoleon, and repeated by several military writers, that the position he had taken up at Waterloo was a bad one, because it afforded no practicable line of retreat, distinctly denied that this was the case, and pointed out that the road to Brussels through the Forest of Soignes was open to him. His words were : " The road to Brussels was practicable, every yard, for such a purpose. I knew every foot of the plain beyond the forest and through it. The forest on each side of the *chausse'e* was open enough for infantry, cavalry, and even for artillery, and very defensible. Had I retreated through it, could they have followed me? The Prussians were on their flank, and would have been in their rear. The co-operation of the Prussians in the operations I undertook was part of my plan, and I was not deceived. But I never contemplated a retreat on Brussels. Had I been forced from my position I should have retreated to my right, towards the coast, the shipping, and my resources. And again I ask, if I had retreated to my right would Napoleon have ventured to follow me? The Prussians, already on his flank, would have been in his rear. But my plan was to keep my ground till the Prussians appeared, and then to attack the French position; and I executed my plan."

While the fight was going on at Waterloo, Grouchy received further orders from Napoleon, written that very morning, instructing him to continue his pursuit of the Prussians in the direction of Wavre, and by four in the afternoon he reached that town, and became engaged with Thielman's corps, which formed the Prussian rear-guard. After a severe struggle the Prussians succeeded in holding their own, and remained in possession of Wavre during the night of the 18th. Early the next morning the conflict was resumed, the opposing forces being still ignorant of Napoleon's defeat at Waterloo; and eventually the

Waterloo June 19th 1815

My Lord

Bonaparte having collected the 1st, 2nd, 3rd, 4th, and 6th Corps of the French Army and the Imperial Guards and nearly all the Cavalry on the Sambre and between that River and the Meuse between the 10th and 14th of the Month advanced on the 15th and attacked the Prussian Posts at Thuin and Lobez on the Sambre at daylight in the morning

*   *   *   *

I should not do justice to my feelings, & to Marshal Blücher and the Prussian Army if I did not attribute the successful Result of this arduous day to the cordial and timely assistance I received from them

*   *   *   *   *

The operation of General Bülow upon the enemy's flank was a most decisive one; and even if I had not found myself in a situation to make the attack which produced the final Result; it would have forced the Enemy to retire if his attacks should have failed and would have prevented him from taking advantage of them if they should unfortunately have succeeded.

*   *   *   *

Wellington

French, who were greatly superior in numbers, carried
the position, and drove back Thielman's corps towards
Louvain.   Very soon, however, the French Marshal
was informed of the result of Wellington's victory,

and at once withdrew to Namur, which in the hurry of the concentration had been left unguarded. There on June 20th he was attacked by Pirch's corps, which had been ordered on the night of the 18th to march from Waterloo to Sombreffe in order to cut off his retreat. The attack was repulsed with heavy loss to the assailants, and the next day Grouchy passed through Dinant and reached French territory without being further molested.

In estimating Wellington's achievements during the brief campaign which ended in the battle of Waterloo, it must be borne in mind that he commanded a mixed force of very unequal quality. The pick of the British infantry who had served in the Peninsular War were still in North America, sufficient time not having elapsed after the conclusion of peace with the United States, to enable the Government to bring these troops back to Europe. With the exception of the German Legion, the Hanoverian contingent consisted of imperfectly trained militia; while the Nassau and Belgian soldiers required very careful handling, believing as they did that Napoleon was irresistible. The following incident, described in Wellington's own language, illustrates the kind of glamour thrown by the French Emperor over some

of the Continental troops opposed to him :—" I had
three battalions of Nassau troops under my command.
I put them in the park at Hougoumont, and expected
that, being old soldiers, they would keep their ground.
But the moment the French began to advance I saw
them waver. It was this which made me withdraw
them and put a battalion of the Guards in their place.
I ascertained afterwards, just what I expected to find,
that the name of Napoleon had beaten them before
they fired a shot ; and that if I had left them there,
the park and probably Hougoumont itself would have
been carried at a rush."

On the morning of the 18th Wellington's force
consisted of 25,400 British soldiers, the German
Legion 6800 strong, about 11,000 Hanoverians,
6000 Brunswickers, 3000 Nassau troops, and 17,500
troops of the Netherlands ; total 69,700 men, with
159 guns. The French army was composed of
soldiers all belonging to the same race and of
excellent quality ; it was 72,000 strong, with 240 guns,
and was commanded by the foremost captain of the
age. That under these circumstances the Duke
should not only have held his own from 11 A.M to
7 P.M., but have succeeded in driving the enemy off
the field of battle at the moment the Prussians were
in a position to take an active part in the conflict, is

a feat almost unequalled in the annals of war. On that particular occasion the British commander certainly displayed greater readiness of resource, tactical skill, and coolness of judgment, than his illustrious antagonist. Wellington was the only general of the first order that Napoleon ever had to encounter, and throughout the campaign the Emperor appears to have underrated his opponent's ability and failed to realise the surpassing bravery and endurance of British soldiers. Some of the French officers who had served in the Peninsula were better acquainted with the fighting qualities of the British army and the Duke's military genius. General Foy told the Emperor that "the British infantry are the very devil in the fight." Soult too warned his master not to be too confident of success. Napoleon replied, "You think, because he beat you, that Wellington is a great general." And when on the morning of the 18th he remarked, "At last I have them : there are nine chances to one in my favour," the Marshal answered —"Sire, I know these English. They will die on the ground on which they stand before they lose it."

After Napoleon's defeat the Allies lost no time in advancing upon Paris. The French frontier was crossed on June 21st ; the following day the Emperor abdicated for the second time, and the provisional

government which replaced him sent commissioners
to negotiate with the British and Prussian commanders.   On June 25th Cambrai and Peronne
surrendered to Wellington ; on the 28th Blucher took
Villers-Cotterets by surprise; and on July 4th a
convention was signed for the capitulation of Paris.
It was stipulated that in three days the French troops
should evacuate the capital, and remove within a week
with their stores and artillery behind the Loire.   The
Allies at once occupied Neuilly and St. Denis, and
entered Paris on July 6th.   Napoleon, who had withdrawn to Malmaison, started for Rochefort at four
o'clock in the afternoon of June 29th, a few hours
before the Prussian soldiers broke into the palace.

With the occupation of Paris, Wellington's service
in the field came to an end, but as Commander-in-
Chief of the Allied Armies in France, his moderation,
sound judgment, and impartiality did much to ensure
lasting peace in Europe.   While he insisted on the
restoration of the art treasures which the French armies
had plundered from the principal Continental cities, he
prevented the destruction of the national monuments
which had been erected in commemoration of French
victories ; and he strenuously and successfully opposed
the demand of the allies of Great Britain for a large
cession of French territory.   His opinion on this

subject is well worth repeating. After pointing out
that France would never acquiesce in the loss of any
of her provinces, and that their forcible annexation
would lead to a state of armed neutrality rather than
a general peace, he remarked : " If we take this large
cession, we must consider the operations of war as
deferred till France shall find a suitable opportunity
of endeavouring to regain what she has lost; and
after having wasted our resources in the maintenance
of overgrown military establishments in time of peace,
we shall find how little useful the cessions we shall
have acquired will be against a national effort to
regain them." Wellington was also instrumental in
adjusting the claims brought against the French
nation on account of the cost of the late war, and the
damage done to public and private property by the
French troops. The commissioners appointed to
investigate these claims were unable to agree, and the
Duke undertook the office of arbitrator ; the result
being that the total charge against France was reduced
from eight hundred millions of francs to two hundred
and forty millions. As Commander-in-Chief of the
army of occupation, he took care that the expense of
maintaining the troops, which fell upon the French
people, should be kept within reasonable limits ; and as
soon as he thought it prudent to do so, he advised the

Allied sovereigns first to diminish the force under his orders, and afterwards to withdraw it, two years before the date fixed by the treaty.

It is almost unnecessary to say that, like most people who do good to their enemies, Wellington was treated with ingratitude by the nation he endeavoured to befriend.   On the occasion of his giving a ball, in June 1816, his house in the Champs-Elysées was set on fire, oil and gunpowder having previously been placed in the cellar.   Fortunately the fire was discovered in time to prevent an explosion.   In February 1818, his life was attempted by Cantillon, an old non-commissioned officer of the Imperial Army.   Napoleon was base enough to leave a legacy of ten thousand francs to this miscreant, in acknowledgment of the service which he had endeavoured to render to France by shooting at the Duke of Wellington ; and a quarter of a century later, Napoleon III. caused search to be made at Brussels for Cantillon's heirs, in order that the money might be handed over to them. The Court, the Ministers, and the chief officers of the French army behaved towards Wellington with a coldness which sometimes amounted to discourtesy.   On one occasion, when he was attending a Levée, the Marshals present barely acknowledged his greetings, and after a short interval, walked away from him in a body. Louis XVIII. had grace enough to apologise for this act of rudeness, whereupon Wellington made the apt reply—" Your Majesty need not distress yourself. It is not the first time they have turned their backs on me."

After attending the Congress of Aix-la-Chapelle in October 1818, and arranging for the evacuation of France by the Allied armies on the 1st of the following month, Wellington returned to England in December and took up the appointment of Master-General of the Ordnance, with a seat in the Cabinet. In July 1815 Parliament had voted him an additional grant of £200,000 for his services in the Netherlands ; and before he left France he was given the rank of Marshal in the Austrian, Prussian and Russian armies, besides other marks of distinction too numerous to mention. This may be regarded as the culminating point of Wellington's career. From December 1818 until June 1846 he devoted himself almost entirely to political affairs. From the latter date up to his death in 1852 the only important public office which he held was that of Commander-in-Chief, to which on the death of Lord Hill in 1842 he had been appointed for life by patent under the Great Seal.

When he commanded in the field Wellington was fully alive to the defects in our military system ; and

it is extraordinary that as a Cabinet Minister, and
afterwards as Commander-in-Chief, he did so little to
remedy those defects, or to carry out much needed
reforms in the organisation and administration of the
army. He considered the material of which the army
was composed anything but what it ought to have
been, but he took no steps to improve it. Yet, as a
man of business as well as a practical soldier, he must
have recognised that, under a voluntary system of
enlistment, able-bodied men of respectable character
were not likely to enter the ranks, at any rate in
peace time, unless the pay and other advantages held
out to them were fairly equivalent to the wages of
civil labour, and unless they were certain of being
treated in a rational and considerate manner. When
Wellington joined the Ministry after the evacuation
of France by the Allied armies he offered no opposition to the inordinate reduction of our naval and
military establishments which then took place. Indeed, he seemed desirous of having as few troops as
possible quartered in the United Kingdom, so as to
avoid irritating the civil population by the presence of
those to whom the nation owed its independence and
prosperity. In his Life of Wellington, Gleig, who was
a personal friend and ardent admirer of the Duke, has
to admit that "it may be questioned, looking to sub-

NAPOLEON'S FLIGHT FROM WATERLOO.

By permission of the Berlin Photographic Publishing Company.

To face p. 176.

sequent events, whether he did not carry the principle
of economy too far. It is certain that he reduced
both the Navy and the Army to such a state as
rendered England virtually powerless if any sudden
call had been made on her military resources. But it
was a game of brag between the Government and the
Opposition, such as will never, we trust, be played
again." What renders Wellington's action in this
matter the more unaccountable is the fact that he was
well aware of the impossibility of upholding our
national rights and interests if England were unpre-
pared for war. In a memorandum written in 1846,
on the subject of the Spanish marriages· and the
hostile attitude of Louis Philippe, he remarked : "We
are not in a state to risk even the smallest manifesta-
tion of angry feeling on this or any other subject.
We must first put our country in that reasonable state
of defence in which it was put after the Seven Years'
War, in which it was before the French revolutionary
war, and in which it ought always to have been kept,
particularly in late years ; but in which it would
almost appear that it had been the object of Government in modern times not to place it." That the
nation would have listened to Wellington had he been
patriotic enough openly to speak his mind, and insist
on the necessity for maintaining the defensive forces

N

of the Empire in an efficient state, is apparent from
the effect produced by the accidental publication of
his letter, dated January 9th, 1847, to Sir John
Burgoyne. He was extremely indignant at this
communication finding its way into the newspapers,
yet there can be little doubt that, had not the country
been thus aroused to a sense of its defenceless condition, no steps would have been taken to strengthen
the Army and Navy. In the letter under reference
the Duke pointed out that our naval supremacy was
not as absolute as it had been at the beginning of the
century, and that it was unwise and unsafe to rely
wholly on our fleet for the defence of the United
Kingdom. He expressed the opinion that, under the
conditions then existing, England would not be secure
from invasion for a week after a declaration of war
with France, he explained the measures which, in his
judgment, ought to be adopted to guard against the
danger, he remarked that he had in vain endeavoured
to rouse the attention of different administrations to
this state of things, and he ended with the following
words: "I am bordering upon seventy-seven years of
age, passed in honour. I hope the Almighty may
protect me from being the witness of the tragedy
which I cannot persuade my contemporaries to take
measures to avert." What Wellington omitted to

mention was the fact that, for a considerable period after his return to England in 1818, he had held high office, that for some years he had been Prime Minister, that for five years he had been Commander-in-Chief, and that up to the resignation of Peel's Government in June 1846 he had exercised a powerful, if not a predominant, influence over the policy of the Conservative party. If then, England was, as he declared, incapable of defending herself against invasion, surely the responsibility rested with him, even more than with his colleagues or political opponents.

A careful study of Wellington's despatches produces the impression that, though perfectly just and impartial in describing the operations in which his troops were engaged, he was somewhat chary of bringing to notice the meritorious services of individual regiments, officers and soldiers. Lord Hill appears to have remonstrated with him on this subject in March 1814; and when Sir Stapleton Cotton in November 1813 urged that a medal should be granted to the cavalry for their services in 1810 and 1812 the Duke replied that in no one instance had it ever occurred to him to apply for a medal for any service performed by the troops. He reported the services in what he thought the clearest and fairest manner to all concerned; and he considered that it rested with the Government, and not with him, to notice the services as they thought proper. His usual answer to those who expressed their disappointment at not having received any mark of the royal favour seems to have been that he had himself never solicited the numerous honours and rewards conferred upon him by the Crown and nation. Writing on this subject to a General Officer in September 1813, he observed: "I recommend to you the same conduct, and patience; and above all resignation, if after all you should not succeed in obtaining what you wish." This, no doubt, was sound advice, though probably rather unpalatable to its recipient, whom Wellington acknowledged to be specially deserving of honourable distinction. Mr. Gleig informs us that the Duke, after his return to England in 1818, associated but little with his old companions in arms. He says: "We have reason to believe that neither Lord Hill, nor Lord Raglan, nor Sir George Murray, ever visited the Duke at Strathfieldsaye; nor could they or others of similar standing, such as Lord Anglesey, Sir Edward Paget and Sir James Kempt, be reckoned among the *habitués* of his hospitable gatherings in Apsley House. The circle in which he chiefly moved was that of fashionable ladies and gentlemen, who pressed themselves upon him, and were flattered, as indeed they had much reason to be, with the notice which he took of them, and by his presence at their parties."

Wellington held very pronounced views on certain points connected with the organisation of the Army; and though these views may now be out of date, they are perhaps not unworthy of consideration, as being based on his long experience as a successful commander in both Asiatic and European warfare. He was strongly in favour of long service and old soldiers. When the Ten Years' Enlistment Act was brought forward, he only supported it on the condition that duly qualified men should be allowed to re-enlist on the completion of their limited engagement. He believed that the efficiency of an army depended as much upon the thorough training and soldierly habits of the men as upon the ability of the officers. On this point Napoleon was of the same opinion, as will be seen from the following extract from "National Life and Character," by the late Professor Pearson :— "Decrès once said to the Emperor in Council, 'I cannot extemporise a sailor as you do a soldier. You turn out a soldier in six months.' 'Taisez-vous,' said Napoleon. 'Such ideas are enough to destroy an empire. It takes six years to make a soldier.' On another occasion he wrote of himself: 'The First

Consul did very good things, he put everything in the right way, but he did not work miracles ; the heroes of Hohenlinden and Marengo were not recruits, but good and old soldiers.' "

Fully recognising the necessity for maintaining our maritime predominance, Wellington was in favour of providing such fortified harbours and bases of supply and refitment as would facilitate and support the action of the fleet. He regarded the Channel Islands as the key of our outer line of defence against French invasion, and recommended the construction of naval bases in Jersey, Guernsey, and Alderney. As regards the home army, he was opposed to the formation of a reserve consisting of men who had completed their term of service with the colours. He considered it to be the proper function of the Militia to reinforce and support the infantry of the line, and urged that it should be raised to a strength of 150,000 men and kept under training for four months every year. With reference to the staff of the Army, Wellington believed in the principle of unrestricted selection, and stated that the only good staff officers he had met with were those who, being thoroughly acquainted with their regimental duties, possessed sufficient natural ability to enable them to apply on a large scale what they had learnt on a small scale. He deprecated the special instruction of officers in staff duties, his words being : "You think that officers ought to be educated specially for the staff. Perhaps you would like to have a staff corps also. That is what they do in France and in other Continental countries, and the consequence is that their staff corps are generally made up of pedants and coxcombs. I am sure that I found the young gentlemen who came to me from High Wycombe* to be pretty much of that stamp."

During the past fifty years great changes have taken place in the organisation of the British Army, and, whether Wellington's advice was sound or not, it certainly has not been followed. In his objection to the formation of an army reserve it will probably be admitted that Wellington was mistaken, even by those who believe that the reserve system now in force is capable of improvement. It adds most materially to the military strength of a nation that its army should be capable of rapid expansion, for in some senses it is undoubtedly true that "Providence is on the side of the big battalions." On the other hand, it seems questionable whether in the present day we are not inclined to exaggerate the fighting

* Formerly there was a Staff College, or, as it was then called, a "senior department," at High Wycombe.

value of large bodies of young and inexperienced
troops, and to imitate too closely the Continental
system of military service, without paying due regard
to our own special requirements. Compared with
armies raised by conscription, the British Army must
always be small, and our endeavour should be to
render it in all military essentials a *corps d'élite.*
History proves that the greatest victories have not
been won by the largest armies, but by the most
capable commanders and the most efficient soldiers.
Alexander invaded Persia with only 30,000 foot and
5000 horse ; Hannibal entered Italy with but 20,000
foot and 6000 horse ; Wellington drove the French
out of Spain with barely 40,000 British soldiers.

The Duke's objection to the special education
of staff officers sounds almost heterodox in these
days of intellectual activity and constantly recurring
examinations. Nevertheless, it was based on principles correct in themselves if not pushed to an extreme, and it was the outcome of his own long and
varied experience as a commander. There can be
little doubt that the value of a staff officer greatly
depends on his being thoroughly conversant with the
details of regimental organisation, and that the duties
of the staff are best learnt on active service. War,
however, is the exception and not the rule ; and in

time of peace the instruction imparted at a staff college, if properly conducted, takes the place of practical training in the field, and tends to develop those intellectual qualities which are needed for the efficient administration of an army. But such instruction is not in itself sufficient. To derive full advantage from it officers must be naturally fitted for the staff; and those who are devoid of the tact, temper, enterprise, resource, and bodily activity which are essential qualifications for staff employ are not unlikely to mistake the means for the end, to imagine that their proficiency as students is a proof of their administrative capacity, and thus to become the prigs and pedants of whom Wellington complained. It follows therefore, that the utmost care should be exercised in the choice of officers for admission into the staff college; and that, while due weight should be given to the possession of a staff college certificate, the responsible authorities should have the power of selecting the most suitable officers for appointments on the staff, whether they are staff college graduates or not.

In bringing these chapters to a close, I will only add that a study of Wellington's life and writings leads me to the conclusion that he has been somewhat overrated as a man and greatly underrated as a commander. Stress is often laid on the strict sense of duty by which he is supposed to have been specially actuated, the inference being that personal ambition had little to do with his efforts to succeed in the tasks entrusted to him. That Wellington was honourable, straightforward, resolute, and patriotic, none can deny; but there appears to be no instance in his military career of his adopting a course where his duty was opposed to his own interests, or of his being called upon to sacrifice the latter in order to carry out the former. In his case the paths of duty and of personal advancement were identical, and it seems, therefore, hardly reasonable to assume that he differed from other great military leaders—such as Cæsar, Marlborough, or Napoleon—in being devoid of that desire for distinction and power which is one of the most potent incentives to exertion. At the beginning of the Peninsular War his own words were: "The ball is now at my foot, and I hope I shall have strength enough to give it a good kick"; and the principal reason he gave for wishing to leave India was that he would be more likely to get on in Europe. Possessed of many admirable qualities, Wellington gained the esteem and confidence, but not the affection, of his soldiers. By nature reserved and unsympathetic—perhaps a little selfish—he regarded his army in the light of a fighting machine. When its

NAPOLEON.

(From the Engraving by Hopwood in the 'Bibliothèque Militaire.')

task was performed and peace established, he ceased
to associate with the officers who had been most
intimately connected with him in the field, and he
did little or nothing to promote the welfare of his
soldiers, or to make the nation understand what a
debt of gratitude it owed them.

The place I should be inclined to assign to Wellington as a general would be one in the very
first rank—equal, if not superior, to that given to
Napoleon.   In estimating the comparative merits
of these illustrious rivals, it may be conceded that
the schemes of the French Emperor were more
comprehensive, his genius more dazzling, and his
imagination more vivid than Wellington's.   On the
other hand, the latter excelled in that coolness
of judgment which Napoleon himself described as
"the foremost quality in a general."   It must
also be remembered that, as soon as Napoleon had
attained supreme power in France, the whole resources of that country and of a great part of the
Continent were at his disposal.   He could raise
enormous armies, incur vast expenditure, and sacrifice large numbers of troops in carrying out his
plans.   Moreover, he was absolutely unfettered in his
selection of the best qualified officers for commands
and staff appointments.   Developing a system of

tactics which proved extremely effective against his Continental enemies, and until his last campaign only opposed by second-rate generals, Napoleon gained victories so decisive and overwhelming that for a time he was believed to be invincible. His presence on the field of battle was regarded as equivalent to a force of forty thousand men.

Wellington's operations, on the other hand, were hampered by the vacillation and timidity of the British Government of the day, his resources were limited, his army was generally outnumbered by the enemy, the reinforcements he asked for were seldom forthcoming, and incompetent generals and staff officers were forced upon him by the Horse Guards. Above all, he must have felt that a single mistake or disaster would probably lead to his own removal from the chief command, and to the termination of the struggle in which he was engaged. Under these un-favourable conditions he never lost confidence. As he remarked before starting for the Peninsula, he was not afraid of the French, although he knew that they were capital soldiers. Believing that their tactics would be unsuccessful against troops steady enough to fight in line, he adopted the extended formation which gave full effect to the accurate fire and resolute courage of his infantry. Throughout the Peninsular War he out-manœuvred and out-fought the ablest of the French marshals. Finally, in the Waterloo campaign, while Napoleon made many mistakes, Wellington made none. His distribution of the Allied troops along the Belgian frontier, his rapid concentration at Quatre Bras in concert with the Prussian army at Ligny, his success on June 16th, his subsequent withdrawal to Waterloo, the manner in which he handled his troops before and during the battle, and the arrangements he made with Blucher for the flank attack from Wavre and for the pursuit of the defeated enemy, prove him to have been a profound master of the art of war. For a brief period the military genius of Napoleon revolutionised Continental Europe ; that of Wellington enabled him to lead his British soldiers, few in number but incomparable in quality, from victory to victory, to march triumphant from Lisbon to Toulouse and from Waterloo to Paris, to overthrow his great opponent, and to establish a peace which lasted for nearly forty years.

INDEX.

LONDON: PRINTED BY WILLIAM CLOWES AND SONS, LIMITED, STAMFORD STREET
AND CHARING CROSS.